All the characters in this book are fictitious and any resemblance to any person living or dead is purely coincidental.

Copyright © Cliff Dix 2025
All rights reserved.

This book is sold subject to the condition that it shall not, by way of trade or otherwise, be lent, re-sold, hired out or otherwise circulated without the copyright holder's prior consent, in any form or any binding or cover other than that in which it is published and without similar condition being imposed on the subsequent purchaser.

Thanks to Ann, for patiently reading again.

ALL INVITED TO A MURDER

Chapter 1

Thursday evening

The two guns lie in their padded box, the lid open. They are both loaded. The round plastic tub of blank cartridges is in the case with them. The spare gun has a loop of red cord tied through the trigger guard. It will hang from a hook near to the prompt desk, in case of a misfire. The polished wooden box lies in the shadows, just like every night, on the props table, behind a scenic flat, just upstage, and out of sight of the DSM at the prompt desk when the play is running.

Sally Jenkins has done her pre-show checks. The stage is set, with its furniture returned to the correct places for the top of the show. The theatre's electrics department has faded up the preset lighting state on stage. The play in music can be heard through the thick, lined, velvet house tabs that divide the stage from the auditorium. Personal props for various actors are in place, the kettle is hot and will just need a quick boil up to make the tea in the pot on the tray of tea things later when act one has started.

Sally sighs. She takes a last look around at the scene. Yes, everything is set. The action will take place in a representation of an opulent traditional country house, all heavy cornices, deep skirting boards, portraits in oils mounted in gilt frames. The bottom of the stairs can be seen through an archway and opposite is the lobby which encloses the front door, built, apparently, of ornate glazed panels, so the audience can catch a glimpse of the comings and goings in and out of the 'house'. There is also a doorway, supposedly leading to the study and another to the dining room.

Upstage, and on the side furthest from her desk, deep armchairs, a sofa and occasional tables frame an impressive fireplace with a small writing desk to one side. For theatrical reasons the furniture incongruously angles away from the fireplace with its brass fire-irons and mantlepiece bearing candelabra and a clock. She checks the clock. Occasionally during the evening she or Edward, her ASM, will alter the position of the hands during scene changes.

She catches sight of Edward in the OP wing. He has finished his checks and is carrying a large grey cat in his arms. It is Rosencrantz, the theatre cat. Nightly he is located and ejected from the stage area ever since he is said to have distracted an audience by walking to the middle of the stage and sitting down to wash himself mid scene during some previous show. Edward strokes the cat as he carries it out of the upstage door into the dressing room corridor. The cat looks around, as it is transported out of harms way for the next two and a half hours.

She goes back to her desk in the prompt side wing. It is little more than a wooden shelf against the black painted wall. Above it various buttons and small breakers surround a metal box with miniture indicator lamps and switches regularly spaced across it. There are Dymo labels above or below lamps and switches, but they are mostly half scratched off or peeling from dog-eared corners where the adhesive is giving up the struggle. There is an impression that at some time, long ago, someone invested in a dymo printer with the intention of smartening the panels, got half-way through the job, and abandoned the attempt. She looks at her watch, and leans in toward the gooseneck mounted microphone, pressing the square red button below it, just as she has done for every one of the last two hundred and thirty-four performances of this play.

"Good evening ladies and gentlemen, this is your half hour call. Half an hour please. Thank you."

It is exactly five to seven. Everything is normal. She phones the front of house manager and gives him 'clearance' to let the public into the auditorium. It is a purely formal phone call. Sometimes she wonders what she has said or done to make the house manager so off-hand with her. She gets a 'thank you' but not even a 'how are you this evening?' or a comment on the weather. Perhaps, she thinks, he is just a cold fish.

Douglas Aiden gets up from his desk, a tidy, ordered, almost sterile desk, picks up a walkie talkie and leaves his office. The street doors are open and the early arrivals are already crowding the bars and foyer. He has been the house manager here for eight years. Shows have come. Shows have gone. 'All Invited to a Murder' will make it to the milestone of a year long run he knows. The advance box office sales ensure that, but he can detect waning interest. They are at the point where managements are privately discussing whether to release the next batch of dates to the box-office for booking rather than when to do so.

He stands by his office door as the audience surges around him and presses the key on the side of his radio, telling the house staff to open the doors to the red upholstered auditorium. Someone comes to him and asks the way to the cloakroom. He has hardly indicated that for them before another wants to buy a programme from him. Sometimes the accepted uniform of dark suit and bow tie is a curse. He is about to make his way to the main stairway to stand observing the flow of bodies, and how his staff are coping. He can detect the doors to the stalls having been opened by a slight thinning as the jam of bodies is allowed to move forward deeper into the building. Looking upward he can see the same effect happening on the main stairway as the doors on other levels are released.

A year will have been too long for this show, he thinks to himself. From the outset it has been a joyless production front of house. A murder mystery doesn't lead to a happy audience. Even full houses do not depart whistling hit tunes from the show to themselves. He fervently hopes that whatever replaces 'All Invited' will be a musical. It cannot be a big show he knows, because the capacity of the venue and the backstage space would work against something with a huge cast or needing a vast orchestra, but musicals usually offer happier punters and that is reflected in the bar take, the kiosk sales and the programme and souvenir income.

He has reached the foot of the stairs. He watches his staff. Tickets are inspected, directions are indicated. Some sales are made over the scattered counters on the ground floor, but the counters are not overwhelmed. He wonders again if he could cut the staffing by a handful thoughout the building without causing too much delay in the process of loading the audience into its seats. He has an accountant's attitude to the venue, he thinks of the audience as so many 'units'. He assesses them by the spend per head. He is no showman, but he has spent enough years in foyers to be aware of how the show affects the income through the tills.

Sally writes the date, and 'Time up' ready to fill the information in on the stage manager's report sheet. Edward appears beside her, brushing grey cat hairs from his stage black shirt and trousers.

"I'm sure that cat is moulting," he says.

Sally grins.

"I think you are stuck with that problem. You're the only one who can catch him. Last time I tried I chased him all over the set and he ended up on top of that bookcase on OP, spitting at me."

"He knows you don't love him."

"I don't mind him... I just don't fuss over him like you do."

"Well there you are then."

"I don't actually 'love' you, but I don't expect you to sit on a bookcase and spit at me," she laughs.

"How do you know what I do when I'm alone because you don't love me?"

"I shudder to think."

"Please don't think," Edward begs her.

He blushes, because he does think about Sally a lot when he is alone, but she doesn't notice in the dark wing.

A door has opened close beside them as they have been chatting, and a middle aged man comes onto the stage from a corridor that runs along the prompt side. Unlike the show crew in their blacks he is wearing rather casual clothes, slacks, an open necked shirt and a worn sports jacket.

"Oh Sally," he says. He has obviously heard the tail end of the conversation and he winks, "have you turned Edward down?"

Sally is cross with herself for discovering she feels embarassed.

"We're talking about Rosencrantz," Edward tells him rather quickly. His haste implies that he didn't want it to be thought that Sally has rejected him.

"That cat," says the new arrival, "loves himself.. and no-one else."

He goes to the tab rope and holds it for a moment, checking the front of house tabs are properly on the stage floor, the 'in' dead. Sally thinks that after the half is a bit late to be checking, but says nothing. After all David Saunders is on the staff of the venue, not the show, and like the house manager, the lighting and sound operators, the box-office staff and usherettes, is not part of the 'company'. 'So perhaps it's nothing to do with me' she tells herself. She knows it is however, and she also knows that she had made sure of the position of the tabs when she was looking around. She could say 'I checked that for you' but she has no wish to score points. She hardly really notices David. She sees him every day, tabs fly in and out as required, he is part of the theatre like the lighting and sound men.

The audience can be heard moving about and talking on the other side of the house tabs. They have arrived in the building through the imposing and ornate front entrance, and been guided into the auditorium either by smart ushers or, if they are regular theatregoers, maybe by following the direction signs to the right level and then the correct side for their seat. They have passed marble pillars and gilt statuettes, varnished wood panels and brightly lit kiosks and bar counters. Now they are seating themselves in red plush tip-ups.

Sally has made her way into the building by the stage door set in a blank and uninviting brick wall in a grimy backstreet that runs beside the venue. Her world is functional. The audience's world is designed to give a sense of rich luxury. She picks up the headphones and says 'hello' down the boom mic attached to them. There is no reply from either lighting or sound. She doesn't expect there to be. It doesn't worry her that the positions are unmanned this close to curtain up, she is confident in the reliability of the long established routine. She takes the cans off and presses the red button again.

"Ladies and gentlemen this is your fifteen minute call. Quarter of an hour please. Thank you."

The three of them stand chatting inconsequentially in the gloom of backstage.

Steven Truss, one of the cast, appears in shirt sleeves, pokes about on the props table, picks up one of the guns and waves it at the trio in a playful way.

"Steven, do put the thing down!" Sally says. She is constantly frustrated by the childish fascination the guns seem to have for most of the cast.

"Yes miss," the actor says, and gives a mock salute before tossing the weapon back into its case.

To take the sting out of her reprimand she says, "If you want to play with one of them, hang the spare on its hook would you please."

Steven picks up the other gun with the hanging cord through its trigger guard and vanishes around the angle of the row of flats. He reappears a moment later without the gun.

"Anyone important in tonight?" he asks.

Sally shakes her head. There have been no reviewers or important members of the profession in the house since the first week of the run. Steven's question puzzles her a little. Would he expect a mid-run visit by anyone? The company would know if the director was coming on one of those occasional check-ups to keep the show up to scratch. Advance news of those visits always seems to leak out. Other than that..

"One night a great impressario will watch the show and recognise my amazing talent. He'll whisk me away to Hollywood and you'll be having to re-cast the part of Paul Burke."

"Meanwhile, while we wait for that great moment, could you go and finish getting into costume."

He shrugs, muttering, "Tons of time yet," and goes off toward his dressing room.

Edward says, "They're all getting bored."

Sally knows he is right. The show is running on a sort of auto-pilot; victim of its own unexpected success and longevity. She nods, realising that she and Edward are suffering the same ennui. Or is it really boredom, she wonders. Some of the cast seem to be falling out with each other frequently these days. There's a distinct atmosphere backstage she thinks. The idea of a 're-cast' seems implausible. They would just shut the show down if one of the company left. Recasting is as unlikely as an impressario whisking Steven, or any of the company, come to that, away to greater things.

She gives the five minute call.

In the dressing rooms the cast are prepared for another performance.

Jessica Campbell dabs at her face yet again with her make up. She is playing the eldest daughter, Rosemary, but she is well aware that she is far too old for the part. Her age shows to her fellow performers in her choice of stage make-up. She is one of very few members of the cast who are still using Leichner grease paint. She squints at her reflection in the mirror as she applies liner around her eyes. It will make her eyes look bigger, though she does realise that as stage lighting has changed over the decades it will also make the artificial 'slap' more conspicuous. She's too old to be changing the techniques of a working theatre lifetime. She concentrates to put the little crimson-lake dot in the corner of each eye.

There is a light knock at her door, which opens immediately to allow Gregory Bradford into her room. She has been allocated one of the better rooms and there is space for a visitor to enter without making the room feel cramped. Sometimes she wishes he would wait for a 'come in'. He plays her onstage husband, though their relative ages, which are hugely evident here in the bright dressing room with its pale gold and white decor, make this relationship highly implausible. Despite this he has called in religiously just before every performance since the show was on its pre-London tour, with a different cast aside from them, all those months ago. She doesn't flatter herself that he is attracted to her, rather, she thinks, he checks in, like a dutiful nephew visiting a rich aunt who he knows has not included him in her will.

"Once more unto the breech, dear friend..." he slightly mis-quotes in forced jocular tone.

'..or close the wall up with our English dead..' her mind continues the line. Yes, that's it, they're all churning their way through this wretched play, night after night, dead from the neck up, dead from the monotony. Though there is occasionally some interest and amusement to be had, she reminds herself, from the slightly vicious sniping among those members of the cast who seem to be involved in two timing their original partners. Sooner or later things may get more lively.

In the prompt corner Sally puts the headphones on again, and is in time to hear the noisy clatter of the lighting and sound operators also doing the same. She winces slightly at the banging as one or other of them positions his microphone on its boom arm with the talk switch turned on.

"Hello you two," she says, and is greeted by both men.

She calls the beginners, "Ladies and gentlemen this is your Act one beginners call, Miss Varley, Mr Truss and Miss Fanthorpe, this is your call."

Idly she opens the prompt copy, though she will find frequently during the performance that she has not turned the pages for long periods, she knows it so well. The pages are mostly old and worn because the book dates back to the original production, and was then used for the try-out tour. When she took over she re-used it, simply blanking where the cast names appeared for calls, photocopying that particular page in each case, and writing the new actor or actresses' name in the blank space on the new sheet before clipping it into the right place in the ring bound script. She didn't have to do this for pages that had calls for Jessica and Gregory, who are still in the cast, so a stranger's handwriting advises her of their calls.

When they first started this run the new pages gleamed whitely and were stiffer and sturdier than the original sheets either side of them. Now hundreds of turnings have worn the new sheets to merge into the dog-eared file of the play.

Douglas makes a quick visual check of the parts of the foyer that he can directly see from his vantage point. He asks his staff by radio if they are all ready. Scattered acknowledgements come back to him, he picks up the nearest internal phone and presses the button for stage.

Sally raises an eyebrow at David Saunders in a casual 'are you ready' way, and he nods, just as the light by the phone flashes.

She lifts the receiver and listens to the house manager saying formally, 'Your House', before thanking him and hanging up.

"Standby houselights and LX cue 1. Standby sound to fade the play-in."

She hears the 'standing-by' replies in her headphones without concentrating on them. She briefly looks round the wings to be sure her cast have arrived. They are there, obedient to her backstage paging and waiting to do it all again.

"Houselights Go."

She sees David hold the tabs rope and flip the brake up so the hauling line is free. There is the barest twitch of the drapes as he does so.

The murmer of voices in the auditorium, which has been a background to the last quarter of an hour or so dies slowly as the lights fade. Last sentences are finished. Final shufflings of seating positions and folded coats mix with the arranging of crinkly bags of sweets.

"Sound Go." and as she hears the music fade she makes a lifting gesture to the tab-man. David pulls upward on the hemp rope and the tabs fly out.

"LX cue 1 Go" she says as David starts to pull, and, as the curtains rise to reveal the lit stage; lighting from the front of house fades up, released by electrics raising the inhibitor, to establish the scene.

She waits for a split second. Sometimes the reveal of the set will produce a round of applause, an acknowledgement of the scene builders' skills or an anticipation of the performance to come. This is one of those nights. She delays pressing the button screwed to her desk that will make the doorbell ring, by a beat, so that the bell is not drowned out by the audience. Judging it exactly from long practice she rings the bell.

David has stopped the hauling line with precision so the sticky tape wound around the rope lines up exactly with the mark on the wall. He eases the brake lever down, locking the curtains in place.

Chapter 2

Act 1

> (*The doorbell rings.*
> *The maid enters stage right. She crosses to the door stage left. She opens it.*)

Maid: Oh, Mr and Mrs Burke. Please come in. Mrs Morgan-Burke will be down very soon. Have a seat in the drawing room. Can I get you some tea?

Paul Burke: No thank you, Molly. I'll pour us some drinks.

"Miss Johnstone and Mr Hattersley, this is your call"

> (*Paul and Wendy Burke enter. Paul goes to the drinks cabinet upstage and pours drinks. The maid exits stage right.*

Paul: Here you are Wendy, drink it up. You're going to need it for a weekend in this place. God I hate this house.

Wendy: It will be fine, I promise.

Paul: And both my bloody sisters here too with their awful husbands, well boyfriends.

Wendy: It will be nice to see them again.

Paul: You mean it will be nice to see Stuart again don't you?

Wendy: (*seeming guilty*) Where do you get these ideas from, Paul?

Paul: I don't think I'm the one who is getting ideas.

Wendy: No, because you've already got them.

Paul: Oh yes, I have ideas, but you have had them, and

have probably acted on them. Don't start airing our dirty washing here, now. The others will be here any moment, if they are on time, though heaven knows your precious Stuart will probably be late, even for his own funeral I should think. We don't want them guessing we are anything other than a loving couple. Mother might pick up on any rumours.

(*The doorbell rings. The maid enters stage right. She crosses to the door stage left. She opens it.*)

Wendy: Quiet! Just put on a good act and no-one will know.

Maid: Oh, Mr and Mrs Fathers. Please come in. Mrs Morgan-Burke will be down any moment. Please join the others in the drawing room. Can I get you some tea?

Rita Burke: Yes please, Molly.
(*she enters with Patrick Fathers trailing behind meekly. Molly leaves.*)
Paul, how nice to see you, and Wendy of course. Where's Stuart?

Paul: Late, of course. I see Molly is still pretending you two are married.

Rita: I expect they've got held up somewhere, the traffic coming out of town was simply frightful. Poor Rosemary, she hated being late even when she was little, remember.

Wendy: Yes, I remember. She had more watches than anyone I've ever met. Hello Patrick, are you well?

Patrick: Fine. You? Are you looking forward to the weekend?

Wendy: Candidly, no. It all scares me a bit.

Paul: Don't be silly, dear.

Patrick: It's not silly, I know exactly what Wendy means. The family is summoned and gathers. Your mother will

	make some major announcement, and her three children will start fighting among themselves. We've seen it before. Last year it was what date we all had to arrive for Christmas.
Paul:	Well the date she chose was hardly convenient for those of us who have jobs.
Rita:	Patrick has a job.
Paul:	Ha!
Wendy:	Paul. Stop it! That's exactly what Patrick meant.
	(*The maid enters with a tray with tea things on, which she places on an occasional table and then leaves*)
Patrick:	Thank you. No not you Wendy, I meant for the tea.

Sally casts a glance at Edward, wondering which of the pair who will drink the tea on stage he has pandered to tonight, trying to remember whose turn it is. All through the pre-London tour the tea was made with common or garden PG Tips, but on arrival in town Beth Johnstone had begun demanding fruit teas like rooibos, strawberry and vanilla. It wouldn't have been a problem, the show budget could absorb the few extra pence a night, except Alan Hattersley, playing Patrick, declared that he just wanted 'a common or garden cupper'. A wrangle had ensued after which a compromise of alternate performances had been reluctantly agreed by both of them, but Sally knows that Edward is steadily working through all the speciality teas he can find on nights when Beth's preferences are allowed to prevail, hoping to find one she doesn't like.

There is a longish chunk of dialogue now with no cues, while the script has the cast explaining the likes, dislikes and frictions between the characters who have so far appeared.

Sally leans back on the chair and swivels it from side to side. 'Autopilot', she thinks, wishing she had brought a crossword to do or a book to read tonight. The headphones hiss gently at her ear and she can tell that both the lighting and sound operators have their mics muted. She hesitates about starting a conversation with them, but in truth there is nothing to say. Despite the length of the run any contact between the resident crew, closetted in their control room at the rear of the audtorium, and the production staff on stage has been purely business. She hopes she isn't appearing stand-offish like she believes the house manager to be. She doesn't think that the resident crew members are, it's just not having any common ground apart from the monotony of a simple show night after night. If you worked in a factory you probably wouldn't find yourself socialising with people from a different department, she thinks. But perhaps you would, perhaps in that sort of situation you'd meet by chance in the canteen.

Edward, passing the corner as he goes about the business of keeping the props in the right places, whispers in her ear, "Peppermint," looks at her for her approval, sees no reaction and shrugs and goes on his way. Sally is not a connoiseur of speciality teas and has no feeling either way about peppermint. He doubts she has ever tried it herself, though the pair of them are conspiring in this enforced tea-tasting that is being imposed on the actors. Neither of them would choose anything other than common or garden tea-bags for themselves.

She watches her cast. She is rewarded by seeing both Beth and Alan grimmace slightly as the action requires them to drink the tea. She feels sorry for Alan, but Beth brought this on herself. 'Stage management one, actors nil.' she thinks, but she knows this petty victory will probably result in another round of between-shows grumbling. She wonders what caused Beth to start to demand speciality tea. She had been undemanding through the rehearsal process and in the provinces. What had made her change? Maybe the woman has just become more self important now she can say she is in a London show.

Chapter 3

Rosencrantz prowls the dressing room corridor. A door is ajar ahead of him. Silently he noses through the gap, easing the door wider to slip inside. Glenda Littlewood is sitting at the dressing table, the mirror in front of her reflects the stealthy motion of the door.

"Hello Rosencrantz," she says quietly, and the cat jumps up onto her lap, and from there onto the dressing table itself where it walks about investigating, and crumpling the magazine she has been reading as its paws turn on the pages. Glenda picks the cat up, sits it back onto her lap, and strokes it. It is ignoring her and extending its head toward her bag inquisitively.

She reaches into her bag with a free hand and takes out a sandwich in a clear plastic triangular box, peeling back the film and extracting a piece of chicken from between the slices of bread of one of the two sandwiches.

"You're not really allowed this until the interval," she tells the cat, as she gives it the morsel. The cat eats the meat filling greedily.

"I don't think they feed you properly," she tells it despite the evidence of its solid weight on her knees. There is a rumbling purr for a few moments as she strokes the animal again, then an attempt on the cat's part to jump down, for long repeated experience makes the cat know that there will be no more food. One titbit each day is an established routine.

"U-huh," she admonishes it, "You can sit here for a bit longer." and she holds it firmly, taking a little comfort from the closeness of a living creature as she waits for her call. She is lonely, and her part is short. She spends too many hours in the solitude of her dressing room thinking. Thinking about life, thinking about her fellow actors.

It strikes Glenda that the animal's fur is exactly the same shade of grey as Jessica Campbell's hair. Despite her unwarranted suggestion to him that the theatre isn't feeding him properly Rosencrantz is a well built heavy cat, also just like Jessica, she thinks. She has the show relay speaker turned well down in her room, but the burbling rise and fall of the script being played out on the stage is a backgound to her musings. She stops her rather critical thoughts about Jessica, and considers Gregory. She thinks him a strange young man. He is playing opposite a woman old enough to be his mother and has done so all through the pre-London tour. Jessica and Gregory are sole survivors of that touring production, but there seems little reason why they should have chosen to stay with the show. Maybe just a case of hanging on to whatever job you have got. She doesn't think that they are romantically involved, though he pays great attention to her, and no-one could have expected the show to run for so long in town. Certainly the management didn't. She remembers how the possibility of a long run was down-played at rehearsals. Now they have all had to rub along together for what seems like a lifetime. She finds it quite hard to recall the insecure days of audition rounds that she and all the cast have been through before this production. Most of them have seized on the security of a less than exciting play with a long run with delight, but the boredom is killing. She knows that most of her fellow cast members have set up permanent homes from home in their dressing rooms. She looks round at hers. The gold and white décor can appear very cold. Her room is almost bare of personalisation, as if she had never expected to stay long. Maybe she didn't, but she feels that she probably should have moved into the space more permanently. Now it seems as though making an effort to do so might tempt a sudden closure of the show. But she spends more time alone in her retreat than the others, well most of the others, having all of act two to herself right up to the curtain calls.

Unlike most actresses she wishes she could skip the curtain call; it would allow her to go home much earlier. It seems silly to wait out the whole second act just to bow and receive some applause.

Adrian, she thinks, has a reverse problem; not appearing till after the interval. But Adrian's wife is in the cast. Anne Birkett only has a minor part. Management, Glenda recalls, assumed that the couple would share a dressing room, but were forced to find them separate rooms. Despite her fairly minor role they agreed and Anne now occupies a tiny room, little more than a cupboard really, on a different floor to her husband. Glenda wonders why. Possibly Anne demanded the status of her own room. Possibly she simply refused to share. Certainly the couple have fallen out, theatricals often do. They are almost never seen together off stage.

Glenda realises that she has hardly spoken to them since the rehearsal period, their paths have not crossed. She regrets this, at least as far as Adrian is concerned. She has heard rumours of a racy past. She thinks that there is probably a racy present. She would like to hear more, possibly from the horse's mouth. Even for a woman of her age there is something disturbingly exciting about Adrian and in any case she would revel in some gossip to mull over in her long enforced periods of waiting.

Rosencrantz is restless. She lets him jump silently down to the floor where he makes immediately for the door, which has swung shut, nuzzling the gap wide enough to leave without any thanks for the scrap of chicken.

As if the cat's exit were a cue she hears Sally's call, "Miss Wynne, Miss Littlewood, Miss Campbell and Mr Bradford, your calls..."

With a slight sigh she gets to her feet and makes her way to the wings, where she climbs the lead-off treads to the off-stage landing which will allow her to make her entrance down the ornate scenic stairway that forms part of the set. The off-stage treads and handrails are plain unpainted pine which has darkened where hands have rubbed along the smooth timber over months of use, in stark contrast to the decorative stairs and banisters that the audience sees.

The actors have moved about during the recent scene. Steven, as

Paul Burke, her son, has been 'outside' with the maid to fetch suitcases. They are returning now as she reaches her position atop the staircase.

From where she is she can see right across the brightly lit stage to the other side, where, in the off-stage gloom, he is waiting for his cue beside the girl. They are little more than shadowy silhouettes, he tall and rather too muscular, she small and slim. Lines are being delivered onstage, but she watches him. He bends closer to the girl and whispers something in her ear. Even in the dark at a distance she can see the girl suppress a giggle, and look up and over her shoulder at him, smiling. They clutch the suitcases and enter, the cases are blatantly obviously empty. It is one of those stupid errors in staging that annoy her. There is no reason not to have stuffed a few old blankets into the cases so they would be convincingly weighty.

The moment of her entrance has arrived. Will she get a round of applause tonight when the audience recognises her? She puts on the voice she has adopted for this part. Confident, haughty and domineering upper class. It carries well to the rear of the auditorium.

Eleanor Morgan-Burke: (entering UR) Patrick, Rita... Ah, Paul, and Wendy, of course. How kind of you to come.

Glenda holds her position on the staircase. It's not how the director blocked the scene, but it forces the other actors to turn upstage towards her, makes her a more commanding presence. 'If I'm only going to appear in act one', she thinks, 'I shall make the most of it'. The audience obliges with a ripple of applause. She feels more a sense of relief than of pleasure. The applause reassures her that at least some of the audience still recognise her.

Wendy: It's very kind of you to ask us.

Rita: Is that what you were saying earlier?

(Paul shushes her with his free hand.)

Paul: You summon us, mother, and we children obey.

Eleanor: You 'children' have never obeyed me...

(*The doorbell rings. The maid hesitates.*)

Paul: Just dump it there, Molly. I'll take it up later.

(*The maid puts the suitcases down and goes to the door to open it*)

Maid: Mr and Mrs Dunsfield, do come in, everyone is in here.

(*Rosemary and Stuart Dunsfield enter.*)

Eleanor: Rosemary. Late as usual.

Rosemary: Sorry mother.

Stuart: That will have been my fault, I'm really sorry Mrs Morgan-Burke ...

Eleanor: Eleanor.

Rosemary: What have we missed then.?

'Here it comes then,' thinks Glenda, 'one day I'm going to corpse over this line'. She studies Jessica for a second. She has clearly used too much No. 9 when she blended it with the ivory No. 5 when making up. Briefly Glenda wonders if the woman picked up No. 8 by mistake. Either way she appears now, as every night, on-stage, ruddy faced. Glenda can see the old fashioned eyelines which the woman has applied.

Eleanor: Rosemary, you're looking very pale. Are you ill?

Paul: Perhaps she's pregnant.

Rosemary: Paul! You never did know how to behave in polite society.

Eleanor: Well? Are you?

Rosemary: Oh no mother, of course not.

Eleanor: No, I don't suppose you are. None of you seem to be willing to produce heirs for the line.

'Poor old Jessica,' thinks Glenda, 'I imagine her chance of becoming pregnant has long past.'

Rita: Patrick and I aren't married, mother.

Eleanor: That doesn't seem to stop anyone these days. Doubtless you and Patrick will be expecting a double room tonight as usual despite that. Molly, go and fetch Annette to take those bags up, the place looks like a hotel foyer.

(*Molly exits.*)

Paul: Is Annette still here then? I thought you said you would be letting her go.

Eleanor: I did think about it after I caught her near my desk, but nothing seemed to be missing, and she could have just been tidying up. Housekeepers do, you know. She's very efficient and there's something strangely familiar about her, have you noticed?

Paul: She looks a bit like Rosemary.

'What nonsense," thinks Glenda, 'It would be difficult to find two women less alike than Jessica Campbell and Anne Birkett. Perhaps the director hadn't read the play when he cast it. This is an anomaly some of the audience will surely spot when the denoument comes round in act two.

Rita: Well be careful, mother, I'd lock my desk if I were you. There's no telling what the staff are up to behind your back and you can't watch them all the time.

Rosemary: What's in your desk anyway?

Eleanor: Really that's what I've called you all here about. Mr. Lowe is coming tomorrow for my signature on my new will.

Paul: A new one? What was wrong with the old one?

Eleanor: I've changed my mind about some... details.

(*Annette enters, listens, and picks up the cases, and goes slowly up the stairs with them.*)

Paul: (*calling after her*) Those are ours, Annette.

Stuart: Ours are still in the car, Annette, it's unlocked.

Rita: What details, mother?

Patrick: I thought it was a simple three way split.

Eleanor: Yes, it was, but I've had a re-think.

Rosemary: You shouldn't be thinking about it all all, mother. It's morbid.

Eleanor: Of course if you were all married or one of you had given me an heir the decision might be different.

(*Paul and Rosemary look at Rita.*)

I'm not trying to force you to get married, Rita. Far from it in fact.

Rita: Oh. You've never have liked Patrick have you! Is that why you're changing things?

Eleanor: Liked? Trusted? We can't chose our childrens' wives and husbands for them, but we can maintain some control over our estates even after we are gone. Our children may even thank us for it in the end.

"Standby LX cue 2," Sally says into the headset microphone, getting a routine 'Standing By' from the control room. When she gives the 'Go' it starts a very long, slow lighting change on the sky-cloth outside the window which goes through sunset and eventually establishes an evening gloom. The stage lighting fades very slowly as this goes on.

Sally watches as Anne re-enters, walks across the scene and off into the wing via the 'front door'. She vanishes from Sally's view as she goes to the props table to collect the other suitcases. Sally hears gentle sounds of movement behind the knuckle of the flattage that hides the actress from her. There's a clunk, followed by a soft metallic click, among these sounds that strikes her as being unusual, though also very familiar. Fleetingly she wonders what the sound was, but she turns her attention back to the performance itself.

When her cue comes Anne re-enters through the door and reappears in Sally's sight taking the suitcases up the staircase. She leaves the cases on the props table on the far side of the stage.

One floor down at street level Reg, the stage door keeper sits in his little kiosk. Visiting cards be-deck the wall beside him, listing taxi firms, take-away outlets, hotels and digs. Behind him the wall is fitted with rows of pigeon holes for incoming post which he hands out to the cast and crew as they come in each day. Sticky labels announce who the post is for. On the upper row the labels are yellowed and peeling, anouncing permanent members of staff and departments. In some places bright coloured Dymo type labels have been added piecemeal. Lower down are the current show cast names, newer, cleaner and in a different lettering style. The evening paper is spread on the plain wooden shelf in front of him, which serves as a counter-top between him and anyone coming through the stage door to make enquiries. At some time the shelf was painted match the maroon of the timberwork around the kiosk, but it has been lent on for so many years that a rough semicircle of bare wood is now visible at the centre of the shelf on the door-keeper's side. Re-decoration of the backstage areas is not a priority. The walls have been a cream colour, but scratches along them tell of bags, cases and deliveries, and the corners all bear the tell-tale dark hue caused by grubby hands passsing by.

Reg knows there will be no curious visitors tonight. This show is not attracting autograph hunters. It is doing solid reliable, though un-spectacular business, but the cast are not 'names', they have no fans. There are a couple of them who are vaguely familiar faces from television roles; Adrian Birkett was once something of a matinee idol, Glenda Littlewood has been in the industry for an eternity, but this is not like the show that preceded it here. That had been a juke-box musical, with a cast that included ageing 'original artists' from the pop world of some thirty years ago. Then the stage door had been frequented by middle-aged fans re-living their teenage crushes for members of the cast. He misses the nightly bustle, and the vicarious thrill of these fans wanting to be allowed in to meet their idols.

Reg sighs and shifts on his high swivel chair. Rosencrantz digs his claws into Reg's corduroy clad knee and remains determinedly in place on his lap. Reg gets hold of the cat's paw and eases the claws out of his trouser-leg before going back to stroking the sleepy animal.

"I wish we could have a lively show in here again," he tells Rosencrantz, "Would you like that?"

There is no response from the cat.

Reg returns to his study of the sports pages. He is warm and cozy in his sports jacket inside the enclosed world of his office, but he is glad of the cat for company.

Glenda thinks that the script reveals her character's intentions with the will too easily. She would prefer her part to have some mystery, or at least suspense, written into it, but she is obliged to launch into the discussion about the changes to the other characters' likely expectations on her death. She uses her long expertise to string out the revelations as much as she can, pointing lines by that tiny pause before the main content that comes so naturally to the experienced performer. If the others feel she is building up her part they say nothing. She doesn't expect them to. She is the centre of attention for this scene, and it is a brief enough moment in the spotlight for her to make the most of it. She plays it in an almost melodramatic style which betrays her age rather more than her preferences.

Sally says, "Standby LX cue 3." in preparation for the chandelier and wall lights to be turned on.

Chapter 3

In his solitary dressing room Adrian Birkett is thumbing through his address book. The worn pages are clamped into an old style Filofax and many are barely readable with age. The entries he originally wrote in pencil have suffered particularly badly. Sometimes he spends a minute or two deciphering one and going over the wording in biro. He has not got into costume yet. He doesn't need to, his character, the police inspector, won't appear until act two. Just like Glenda he finds himself obliged to be in the theatre for the whole duration of each performance, despite only being seen by the audience for half of it.

He is amusing himself as always by reading the address pages, and refreshing his memory of the the girls whose names are carefully written there. The sheer quantity of people that any actor comes into contact with in a working life is impressive, but Adrian is skipping over the business contacts, the agents, the directors, the newspaper reporters, and pausing only at his conquests. He smiles gently to himself as he recalls individual details of his numerous liasons.

This introverted attempt to remember all about a succession of affairs dating right back to his youthful days in acting school is partly a reaction to the tense atmosphere that has existed between him and his wife for many weeks.

His mind wanders to all those actor friends whose marriages have broken up. Sometimes the split has come due to one or other partner having started an affair with someone else. There may be something about the backstage world that encourages infidelity, he thinks. Frequently, he remembers, there are break-ups where a new partnership has been the result of two people ,who are acting being a couple in a show, becoming a couple in real life. There is little likelihood of that scenario for him in this production, but there is a theatre world out there and other venues in the city.

In his case Anne has turned cold on him mainly because of his habit of looking wistfully back at the days of his, largely misspent, youth and the girls he knew then. Just like he is doing now, he realises, but he feels no guilt at his absorbed recollecting. He turns another page and a name springs out and shocks him with a pang he hadn't anticipated and doesn't really expect.

Naomi Johnstone. Was that really her surname? They called her 'Bunny', he remembers. Closing his eyes he can conjure up an image of a cute, almost naive, teenager. She is wearing a crop-top and rather brief shorts. They are heading out of the little harbour in his speedboat. The summer sun is dazzling as it reflects off the wavelets. He remembers pushing the throttle forward so the small craft bounces across the water faster and faster. The boat is almost flying, actually leaving the water from time to time as it skips on the choppy estuary. Bunny is squealing delightedly. His concentration is all on her, on the curves under her tight white top and the display of bare flesh below, down, past her navel, to the cheekily low waistband of her shorts and her long bare legs. He remembers that he was thinking about how they had been in bed the previous night.

Then suddenly, mid-way through flicking her loose brown hair away from her laughing face, she had shouted 'Look!' and pointed almost straight ahead.

The seemingly huge red and black mass of the marker bouy, with a light atop it and the number '7' painted on its sloping sides had been just feet from the bows of his speedboat. He remembers spinning the wheel of the craft as it hurtled toward the obstacle, the gut-wrenching fear as the boat turned sharply, the rudder sliding sideways through the water instead of gripping it, a grinding as they brushed the side of the bouy with the underside of the heeling hull, and Bunny, flailing for a handhold, flying though the air and out of the boat. Grabbing for the throttle to cut the engine and the certain premonition as the girl was slipping under the craft toward the screaming propellor.

He remembers the funeral. Black clothed figures round the hole in the ground, and how he stayed well back, away from the accusitive looks from the girl's mother, father, and a little girl he assumes was a sister. Funny, he'd not thought about Bunny for a long while, blocking out the shock behind happier memories of other conquests. For the briefest moment his recollection of the child by the graveside reminds him of Beth Johnstone, the same dull, sad, expression directed at him. 'She's a strange woman' he thinks to himself of the actress. Presumably it's just the co-incidence of the same surname that has caused him to think of her while musing about Bunny.

The memory has upset him more than he cares to admit. Months, even years have gone by without his day-dreaming causing him to re-visit that day on the boat.
Hesitantly he flicks the page with Bunny's address on it back and forth, checking if anything is on the back of it, then, decisively, he tears it away from the six shiny steel rings that clamp it, and out of the book, screws it up, and throws it in the bin under the dressing room shelf.

He is starting to think about his wife and their split again, and consciously pulls himself together to stop from sliding down into a self-pitying mood. She is upstairs in her dressing room, he is down here in his. Somehow it is never her presence that he misses.

He turns another page; ah! Barbara, the dancer. That was a lively and happy affair. He settles into reminiscence again as act one of the show murmurs gently from the speaker screwed to his dressing room wall.

Eleanor: I have made my decision. I will explain it all to you tomorrow when Mr Lowe is here, but none of you will be destitute, it's just a slight re-arrangement.

Rita: I do hope you are going to be treating us all fairly, mother. I'd hate to think Rosemary was getting preferential treatment because she's married, or the youngest, or Wendy's having a bigger cut because of being your favourite, Paul's, wife or....

Rosemary: Rita! Stop it. You're being very greedy. It doesn't suit you, it's not becoming behaviour.

Rita: Well it's always been the same. Paul gets the best of everything because he's the oldest, and you get special treatment because you're the youngest, and I get the dregs.

Eleanor: It seems to me that it's getting very gloomy in here. Wendy, do turn the lights on for us please.

(*Wendy goes to the light-switch and turns on the chandelier and the wall brackets.*)

Sally says "LX cue three go" and the practical lights snap on, accompanied by a brightening of the general lighting state. She returns to her rather casual slouch at the prompt desk, knowing that there are no more cues for the control room till the end of the act.

Paul: I think that now you have let on that there is to be a change you should tell us the news at once. If you leave it to tomorrow some people will be fighting about what they guess might happen for the rest of the evening.

Eleanor: I had hoped Mr Lowe could have told you. I didn't want all this unpleasantness.

Rita: Maybe you should have left it all alone. But tell us the worst then. What have you done?

Eleanor: I don't have to tell you anything, but it seemed polite to let you know what to expect, which I was going to do tomorrow. But if you you are all going to make a scene about it I shall just deal with Mr. Lowe, and you can wait until I am dead to find out.

Paul: Mother, it would be much better for us to know. We all have responsibilities, you know.

Rita: When have you ever been responsible about anything?

Eleanor: Enough! I'll tell you, but I'll tell you because I intended to anyway, not because you are bullying me.
I have had Mr. Lowe revise my will to match your seniorities.
There will be a few fixed sums to go to people like Molly, Annette...

Rita: The Annette you were going to dismiss a few days ago?

Eleanor: (*firmly*)... Molly, Annette, and Mr Appleyard who does the garden of course. After that, and some money to the church, the bulk of my estate gets divided among you three, my children. Paul gets half, you girls each get half of the remainder.

Rita: But that won't be enough for Patrick to.... Oh damn you mother! Why couldn't it have stayed a three way split?

Eleanor: Perhaps I didn't want it to be enough for whatever Patrick thought he was going to do with my money. I'm leaving my money to my children, not to whoever they have been foolish enough to pair up with. What Patrick wants, or needs, is of no interest to me. It isn't up for discussion. Now I am going to change for dinner. Seven o'clock as usual, don't be late.

(*Eleanor exits up the stairs.*)

Glenda makes her way to her dressing room. She has plenty of time for the costume change and she does not hurry. She half hopes she will meet some other member of the cast or crew on her way, just so she can exchange a few words other than the script with them, but as usual no-one is around. It is just her luck, she feels, that the script has her off-stage at points in act one when the rest are mostly busy appearing, and then repeats that arrangement when she is competely free for the whole of act two.

Rita: We have to stop her signing it tomorrow.

Paul: Do we? Why?

Rita: Well thank you Mister 'I'm all right Jack'. Because your share has just gone up and Patrick and I will be left struggling.

Rosemary: Struggling?

Rita: Patrick has a lot of commitments.

Paul: Does he now?

Patrick: Rita, they don't have to know.

Rita: I think they do now dear. We need the guarentee of the money because of Patrick's gambling debts. We're just about holding off his creditors on the eventual promise of mother's money, but if there turns out not to be enough of it...

As the scene continues the script arranges for each couple to be left alone while the others go off to change for dinner. The audience is allowed an insight into the relationships as they have these private moments together.

Steven Truss and Tessa Fanthorpe, playing Paul and Wendy, have left the stage. They head for their respective dressing rooms. Tessa turns into hers, leaving Steven to continue along the passage, but he passes his own room and goes up a flight of stairs, stopping eventually outside and tapping on the door of, Julia Varley's room. She opens it, sees him standing outside, and giggles. He thinks she is very cute in her maid costume.

"Steven, you should be getting changed," she says, mock scoldingly.

"There's tons of time," he presses her into her room and the door just has space to close behind them both. The little room is even smaller than the one Anne Birkett has been given and they are crowded together. Julia has settled into her private domain with a few make-up items on the shelf under the mirror, her coat and street clothes on hangers on the short rail enclosed in a hanging space on one wall and an extensive collection of post cards, greetings cards and family pictures plastering the remaining walls. Her youth and relatively new career are more painfully obvious in the quantity of 'good luck' cards she has retained and displayed. Even now she is still revelling in the novelty of such things and her room reflects this. The room may be little more than a glorified cuboard, but Julia feels some pride in occupying it. At this rather early stage in her career she feels it says much that she has her own room in a London theatre in a long running show. Her pride ignores the quirk of the venue that it has more numerous small dressing rooms than might be expected, and comparatively few large chorus sized ones. This is one of the constraints that Douglas was contemplating as the house opened.

Like almost all the cast Julia's dressing table also bears a newspaper, and a puzzle book folded back on itself at a partly completed crossword. There's a well loved cuddly toy perched on one end of the work surface.

Pushed with her back against the shelf by Steven's entry into her room she is half sitting on the room's crude table as he presses closer to her. He puts a hand on each of her shoulders.

"Come for a meal tonight after the show," he suggests.

She knows that he has been building to this for some time so she is not hugely surprised. He had first started being conspicuously attentive to the young actress quite early in the run, though only in the past fortnight has he been quite so openly trying to move the casual relationship onward. He is too old for her, but his personality is appealing, his conversation jocular, and his attentions flattering and gentle. All the previous liasons she has had have been brief flings, a bit of fun, usually starting quickly after she met the man. She is unused to this slow-burning build up. It makes her wary, as she wonders if it implies that he wants a long term relationship. She knows that she doesn't, well at least not with Steven. Her intuition tells her that below the attention and smooth talk lies a harder and more selfish Steven. But she is unattached at present and feeling rather neglected.

"That would be nice," she tells him, after hesitating a moment.

"I'll come and find you after the show," he promises, and he leans forward to kiss her very gently. There's a whiff of theatrical make-up and he leaves, sideling his way rather clumsily out of the cramped doorway. Somehow his exit, clumsily struggling with the door, humanises him and emphasises his age, disguising what might otherwise show as a predatory interest in the younger member of the cast. She sits in front of her mirror and checks that the peck has not smudged her make-up. The worn soft toy panda stares at her with unblinking glass eyes.

"No Andy," she says to it, "I don't know either." There is no response from the toy, but she hardly expects it. Andy Panda has been a silent recipient of her confidential hopes and fears and occasionally anger through all her many relationships now. It was a gift from an early flame, so long ago now that the association with a former partner has faded and is mostly forgotten. The panda's face seems a mute, innocent appeal 'Nothing will shock him,' she thinks silently of the stuffed animal. Andy is an ideal confidant for her.

Anne Birkett is in her room thinking about her husband. She knows that he will not have started dressing and getting made up yet. She knows that he has always been quick at the preparations, and will probably not start until well into the interval. Vaguely she wonders if he gained his ability to dress quickly from his numerous affairs. There must have been times when he needed to leave before husbands returned to catch him. Despite her bitterness at the way he has treated her during their marriage she smiles at the thought of Adrian making hasty escapes like a character from a comic film or stage farce and envisages him climbing from windows clutching his trousers over his arm pursued by an irate husband.

She knew he was a bit of a playboy when she married him. Knew she was just another in a succession of conquests, but she had thought, as several others before her probably had, that she could tame him, hold on to him, and that their shared profession would be the thing to turn them into a stable couple. What was once attraction has soured for her through disappointment, to dislike; from hostility, now to the edge of hatred. It would be best to be rid of him by almost any means.

Hindsight is a terrible thing, and now she knows that all that the world of theatre gave their marriage was greater opportunities for Adrian to have short affairs with other girls in the casts. Musicals and pantomimes were the most troublesome for Anne, offering Adrian dancers and chorus girls in quantity, but in all cities other adjacent and local theatres will always include those which are running shows with leggy girls for him to chase.

Then there was the accident too. She thinks over what she knows. Adrian never talks about the speedboat or what happened that day, but sometimes he must think of it. She knows he can be hard and cold, selfish and unfeeling, seducing the girls for his own pleasure, but surely there must be remorse about the girl in the boat. Gentle probing in the early days of her marriage to him only produced a stone wall, a solid refusal to even acknowledge the incident, let alone talk about it. What snippets she does know have come from accidental mentions by a few of Adrians long standing acquaintances, usually swiftly bitten off and curtailed, almost as if they were in fear of his reaction to any mention of the event.

Anne has only found out about her husband's address book since this show opened. He had never hidden it, but it was chance that led to her seeing it open on the kitchen table one day when he went to answer the door. It is galling to think that he keeps the record of all those other girls, and spends time thumbing through and remembering them. A quiet vengeful anger, which started as a form of jealousy before morphing into hatred, has built in Anne, growing day after day. Her visit to the props table every performance shows her the guns each time. She realises she is becoming more fascinated by them daily. Now when she is in that wing, hidden from view, she has taken to handling the firearms, holding them and feeling their tactile weight. It is just a fantasy. She can think of no way that she could get away with shooting her husband, and in calmer, more sanguine moments she doesn't think he is worth going to prison for.

No, she will get a divorce.

But it would be nice to really punish him.

Jessica and Gregory leave the stage to change for dinner. They have done this so many times now that they are hardly thinking about the performance, having played Rosemary and Stuart Dunford since the pre-London tour. As the only two members of the cast who were part of the original production they both feel they deserve some acknowledgement for their seniority. Jessica privately admits to her qualification for 'seniority'. She may be playing Glenda's daughter, but she is aware that they could swop roles without any comments on their appearances being made. Her stage husband could easily be mistaken for her son. In more depressed moments she wonders whether some members of the audience are confused. The age difference has become increasingly obvious over the long months since they first set out on the tour of this show. Nothing that she tries, to give the impression of youth to her appearance, has any effect. She would probably be hurt if anyone were to suggest a lighter touch with her make-up. For her the make-up is a mask to hide behind and, ignoring the script, she strives to achieve a healthy rosy glowing look each night.

The couple's exit leaves the stage to Beth and Alan.

Patrick: My god, Rita, what am I going to do?

Rita: We'll find a way to get her to change her mind, I promise.

Patrick: I don't see that happening if she's got the solicitor coming round in the morning.

Rita: I'll have to persuade her. It was all going to come to a head anyway. You couldn't keep fending them off saying that you were expecting an inheritance while she was still alive for much longer. I'll just have to come clean and explain to her how much you owe.

Patrick: I don't think she's going to be very sympathetic to an appeal for help with gambling debts. If she'd left well alone and had the decency to die quickly we could have managed.

Rita: Patrick! That's my mother you are talking about.

Parick: A mother you say always ignored you in favour of your big brother and little sister.. and she's doing it again now.

Rita: I don't wish her dead though.

Patrick: But I need the money.

Rita: Don't remind me. Those people you owe seem really nasty. I heard the way they were talking to you. They're going to come collecting one day.

Patrick: I'm likely to wake up with no kneecaps if they do come looking.

Rita: Darling, you've been a stupid, stupid boy, but I will sort it, I promise I will. If she doesn't agree to keep the will as it is we'll just have to find a way to stop her signing the new one.

David Saunders comes through the door in the downstage corner of the prompt-side wing, behind where Sally is lounging. She hasn't called him yet for the interval curtain, it is still some way off, but he has finished the chapter in the book he is reading in his office hide-away, buried slightly lower than the stage in a space next to the proscenium arch. Periodically when this happens he wanders onto the stage to watch a bit of the show from beside Sally. He likes Sally. From his point of view she is the nicest member of this company. Actually he has had hardly any contact with the actors. Sometimes as the curtain calls are being taken and he looks along the line of players from the side and he realises that he knows nothing about any of them. He knows little about Sally either, having only exchanged a daily 'Hello', possibly a 'How are you?' and 'Fine thanks' reply that means little and doesn't indicate any real interest in the other person's welfare. It is just a formula. But David would like to know her better. Much better. Over weeks she has unwittingly become a small fantasy for him which he has no expectation of ever coming true. Still it is pleasant to stand close to her in the warm darkness of off-stage. The play continues just the other side of the plywood flattage. He hears the cast giving their lines, and even he, an occasional visitor this far ahead of the act one curtain, feels a comfortable familiarity with the script from repeated listening to the show as a background being broadcast over the show relay speakers.

Sally senses his presence as he stands looking down at the back of her head and she turns, seeing who it is, before giving him a quick flash of a smile and turning back to face the prompt copy. It is a smile of recognition, nothing more. Having people in the wing behind her tends to make her follow the script conspicuously. It is a silly, half guilty reaction to being observed. She remembers starting to write furiously when teachers patrolled the aisles at school and approached her from behind. Tonight she hasn't turned the page for some time, and idly, almost surreptitiously, flips though to catch up. She calls Steven and Tessa, Jessica and Gregory back to the stage from their costume changes ready for Beth and Alan to exit. She doesn't refer to the page of the prompt copy she has turned to to do this. She knows her script as well as, if not better than the cast.

Calls made she adjusts her headphones. Some of her hair catches in the headband so an untidy loop of it sticks up on the back of her head. David wants to reach out and smooth it down for her, but he doesn't. It would be an intimacy she might reject and he wants to avoid rejection.

Another chunk of the play passes and then they are coming towards the end of the first half. Sally calls the rest of the cast, so that they are all in the wings or onstage except for Adrian. She puts electrics on standby for the end of the act, tells sound to standby with the interval music, nods quizzically at David, who nods back to show he's ready for the curtain. Sally goes to collect the gun and comes back to her desk.

Rita: ... and I'm surprised that you've managed to put up with working for my mother for so long, Annette.

Eleanor: Rita, sometimes you can be the rudest person I know!

Rita: Well it's true, mother. Why would anyone carry on in a house like this?

Patrick: (*aside to Rita*) Perhaps Annette thinks she is in line for a big share of the will. She might be if she's getting a lump sum. We don't know how much that might be. Once the new will is done we're going to be short changed.

Rita: Except for Paul who will be quids in.

Eleanor: Annette, can you go and shut the porch door please while my children indulge in this unseemly squabble.

(*Annette goes out through the hall*)

Anne is offstage once more, alone and next to the remaining gun. She has several moments before she has to re-appear. She holds the spare again, turning it over and studying it and opening and shutting it quietly, before replacing it with reluctance and making her way back into the scene where Glenda is sending the other actors to the dining room.

Eleanor: ... and I'll join you in the dining room in a minute.

> (*They all exit, upstairs or towards the dining room. Eleanor goes into the study. A pause.*)

There has been a flurry of movement. Anne has re-entered, only to leave again almost at once. Steven and Tessa exit through one doorway, Beth and Alan up the staircase. Jessica and Gregory pause on the stage, before following them. Once off-stage and out of sight of the audience the cast hurry to their positions for re-entering. They brush past each other in the wings. There is a bottleneck on the lead-off treads from the stairs. At stage level Julia is almost shoving to ensure she can enter first, as she must. Unheard by the audience there are hastening footsteps as those that are to re-appear ready themselves. Those not already 'dressed for dinner' are doing quick changes of costume. The end of act one is approaching.

Sally can just see Glenda as she leaves the stage. Once the actress has gone she waits for a count of three, points the pistol straight up and pulls the trigger. The single loud shot breaks the momentary silence. Some of the audience jump. In his dressing room Adrian hears the bang, partly over the show relay speaker, and partly live as it echoes along the stage level passageways. Other cast members can hear it too. Some are heading to their rooms, some descending the lead-off treads. Some are ready and waiting to re-enter. Glenda pauses at the props table and touches the spare gun. It is almost a superstition. She can hold the prop that is supposed to kill her character. Not the actual one, because Sally is holding that, but one the same. She shakes her head at the nightly stupidity. She knows that there is no logic to her action. Resolving to break the habit she lets the firearm go back to dangling from its cord and strolls out of the prompt side door into the corridor and heads to her dressing room. She finds this moment in the play unsettling. Not particularly because it signals her character's death, she has no problem with that, but because for a brief few seconds everyone seems to be moving about, off-stage and out of place. The actors have all left the stage and every night there is a mêle as some try to re-enter and some hurry to their rooms for the interval break. She is glad that most of this disturbing movement is on the opposite side. Edward is somewhere in the midst of this, readying himself for the interval re-set. The only fixed point seems to be Sally, gun raised in her hand, standing next to her desk.

Glenda dislikes the confusion. All her training and expectations lead her to believe that the wings will be full of twilight stillness and calm. It is this calm and controlled feeling that she thinks is an essential part of the theatre world. No matter how much activity is going on backstage, or how frantic it may be, it should have a pre-determined order about it she feels. And yet somehow this tail end of act one is fraught with the movements. She is aware of another change that this moment of activity causes. She thinks of herself as the star, after all she has top billing, and all her previous experience has re-inforced this as everyone from stage-hands to cast members usually make way for her when she moves about. At this point in the show the hurry means she doesn't get that preferential treatment. She counts herself lucky to be able to slip out to her room by a route that is hardly used by her peers.

She hears members of the cast hastening to cross the stage, footsteps broadcast over the backstage speakers in the passageway leading to her room, and, after a pause, a scream as her murdered corpse is supposedly discovered out of the audience's sight through the door to the study, running feet coming on to investigate the cause of the scream.

Sally gently lowers the smoking gun to point downward and says, "Lx cue four, go," and the scene fades to blackout. She flags her free hand downward at David who is by the tab rope, with the brake off and his hands high above his head ready to pull downwards. Obediently he pulls. The tabs fly in and she is saying, "Houselights and preset.." Lights come up on stage, seeming over-bright after even such a brief period of blackout. Sally asks sound for the interval music, writes 'time down' for the first half in her record, before turning her attention to the interval change.

Chapter 4

The audience is noisy tonight through the thick velvet of the house tabs. There seems to be no logical explanation for the variations in the way an audience behaves. David pulls the release on the safety curtain and the iron rattles down its tracks till it is slowed and sinks gently the last few feet to an accompanying hiss of air. The noise from the auditorium fades as the iron completely blocks the archway between the stage and the house. The side facing the audience is boldly lettered 'Safety Curtain'. Much smaller old lettering along the bottom advises that the Theatres Act requires this safety curtain to be lowered and raised at least once each performance.

Now under a basic working light state Edward and Sally are resetting ready for act two. Edward is crossing and re-crossing the stage with the various suitcases that have arrived in the previous act and stacking them back onto the props tables in the right order for the next performance. He clears away tea things from the side table and replaces decanters and glasses in their normal positions after refilling them. He adjusts the furniture and plumps up the cushions before hurrying away backstage to the stage management's room to wash up the used crockery and glasses.

Sally walks round the stage checking, pausing by the hallway clock to open its face and wind the hands on to show the audience that time has passed.

Returning to prompt side she collects the spare gun and puts it in the case. She opens the one she has just fired and ejects the used cartridge into the bin below her desk before shutting the weapon with its duplicate in the polished wood box. With the briefest of checks she hurries to the stage management room just behind the stage and locks the guns in the steel cabinet that stands there. She is back in plenty of time to announce 'Act two beginners please.' As she does this David presses the button and, with a muted rumble of electric winch, the iron rises again, its daily legal obligation fulfilled, so the audience is looking at the house tabs once more. Douglas, prowling his auditorium amid the interval trade, is aware of the iron vanising behind the ornately swagged velvet and gold tassels above the proscenium arch. Half the audience probably completely fail to notice the nightly ritual, either out of the auditorium at the bars, or queueing for toilets or ice creams.

Sometimes Adrian arrives on stage before the Act two beginners' call. He has done so tonight. Frequently he will murmur suggestive chat-up lines in Sally's ear. They range from flattery to outright smutty inuendo. She knows his reputation and largely ignores him. Tonight he is standing behind her chair gently massaging her shoulders. She has to admit to herself that he is doing it very well. She is surprised by her response to this tactile closeness. She is pleased that he isn't saying anything now, just rubbing her shoulders, running his hands back and forth across them and pressing his thumbs gently into the muscles. She says, 'Mmmm' very faintly, surrendering.

David, by the rope, watches, and feels jealous feelings boiling inside him. He has not dared to approach Sally, much less touch her. This actor, who seems old enough to be her father, is being allowed to caress her. It seems unjust to him. It annoys him. It will be something to torment himself with overnight once he gets home.

With the interval over the curtain rises and the scene is as before, though some furniture has been moved and the lighting, called by Sally as the act starts as cue five, implies late afternoon.

Act 2

Scene: later the next day. Detective Inspector Palmer has placed a table to one side of the room and sits behind it interviewing each suspect in turn. As the curtain rises Annette is standing in front of him being questioned.

Anne arrived onstage in response to the act two beginners' call in time to see her estranged husband massaging Sally's neck. Like David she was strangely annoyed by this blatant familiarity, unlike David it has not caused jealousy. Jealousy implies wanting something, and Anne wants nothing from him. But the actions she has seen have fanned the hidden hate that simmers inside her. Now they deliver their lines to each other, hiding any feelings.

Palmer: How long had you worked for Mrs. Morgan-Burke?

Annette: Three, nearly four years.

Palmer: And is it true that she sacked you recently?

Annette: She said she was going to, but she changed her mind.

Palmer: Why was that?

Annette: There was some suspicion that I had opened her desk, but I hadn't.

Palmer: And Mrs Morgan-Burke accepted that?

Annette: Oh yes. It was just a misunderstanding.

Palmer: Did you like working here?

Annette: I wanted to work here so I kept applying, eventually I got the job. I've always felt, I don't really now how to explain it to you, a.. 'connection' with Mrs Morgan-Burke and the family.

Palmer: With all the family?

Annette: Most of them.

Palmer: Tell me about them all.

Annette: Well there's Paul and Wendy, Paul's the eldest son,

	and his wife is, no was, probably Mrs Morgan-Burke's favourite. But I don't think Mrs Morgan-Burke ever knew about Wendy's affair with Stuart.
Palmer:	Stuart?
Annette:	Rosemary's husband, the youngest daughter. It was a big scandal among the children when it came out. I don't think Paul and Wendy ever really got back together properly afterwards.

The irony of discussing infidelity with her estranged husband as part of the show every night is not lost on Anne, though she has the impression that Adrian is unaware of it. Nightly in this short scene she has looked for any reaction to the script content from him and failed to find it.

She ploughs on with her lines.

	I suppose you wouldn't. In fact I'm not sure that the affair is over. Mrs Morgan-Burke would have been very angry if she knew, perhaps she just found out and ... Anyway, there's them, and there's Rita and Patrick, but they're not married.
Palmer:	And that's everyone in the house?
Annette:	Apart from myself and Molly, the maid, and Mr Appleyard the gardener, but he never comes inside, just works in the grounds and the greenhouse.
Palmer;	And you can't think of anyone who'd want to harm your employer?
Annette:	She'd just told everyone that she was changing her will, so some of the family were worried that their share would be reduced. Mr Lowe came this morning to see to the signing, but of course he was too late. I suppose that means it didn't get changed?
Palmer:	Thank you, that's very helpful. Can you send Molly in

	please. By the way would you have been better off under the new will do you know?
Annette:	(*turning to go*) I don't think either version gave me what I was entitled to.
	(*she leaves* *Molly enters after a pause. She is crying.*)
Palmer:	Please don't upset yourself Molly, it's just a few routine questions so I can get an idea of what has happened.
Molly:	I'm sorry sir, it's just thinking about her, like that.
Palmer:	Ah yes, of course, it was you who found the body wasn't it?
	(*Molly sniffs and nods*)

These interviews carry on for much of the act, as the detective extracts the backgrounds and where each individual was at the time of the murder. Sally gives backstage calls as each member of the cast's appearance nears.

Molly:	It was horrible.
Palmer:	Yes I expect it was a shock. Tell me did anyone have a grudge against your employer that you knew about?
Molly:	No, no. It was supposed to be a nice family gathering....
Palmer:	And the family all got on?
Molly:	Well I think some of them didn't like Mr. Fathers very much, but then he did always seem to be short of money, and trying to borrow from people, and Mrs Morgan-Burke was saying she was changing her will. Some of them seemed a bit cross about that, and Rita can get quite forceful when she doesn't get what she wants.

Palmer:	She wasn't going to get what she wanted then?
Molly:	I don't know, but there was a lot of talk among the family about stopping Mrs Morgan-Burke from changing her will, as I said she was going to, you know. Mr Lowe was coming today to sort out the signing.
Palmer:	Do you know where the gun came from?
Molly::	Oh yes, it was old Mr Morgan's. It lived in the drawer in the study.
Palmer:	So everyone knew it was there. I suppose it wasn't locked up.
Molly:	Locked up? No, of course not. It wasn't dangerous. The children used to play with it occasionally when they were little.
Palmer:	You've been here that long?
Molly:	Yes, nearly twenty years now, but I was very young when I started.
Palmer:	Did the children have any friends who might have known about the gun?
Molly:	No. I don't think anyone ever visited. It was rather sad for them really, Must have been lonely for them really. No one else ever came in the house apart from the family and we servants. Though there was the baby, but that got taken away.
Palmer:	Baby?
Molly:	I suppose it doesn't matter now, but we were all sworn to secrecy. Mrs Morgan-Burke had another child, but it was given away. I suppose she might have kept it if it had been a boy, but ... Anyway no-one on the staff was allowed to mention it and I don't think the children knew. They were too little at the time. Of course

there's no-one else left from those days.

Sally grimaces in the corner and turns another worn page of the prompt copy. 'No one left from those days' she thinks...the line is a nonsense. Julia would need to be twenty years older for her character to have been working for the family in the way the script implies. Idly she wonders whether the actresses in the original production, and then on the pre-London tour, were similarly miscast for the character's age. Their names are preserved on the front pages of the script she is using, pages she did not bother to revise when she remade the book. One day she might look them up in a casting directory to see. But she knows that she won't. Like all such vague ponderings she will forget before she next finds herself with time heavy on her hands. Idly she turns back to the front of the file, keeping one finger in the page that the performance has reached, to the page headed 'Cast in order of appearance'. A quick scan of the names shows she is right. No names that she recognises spring out at her: *Maid... Nicole Wade, Paul Burke... Laurence Drover, Wendy Burke... Abigail Sander, Rita Burke...* She gives it up. No mental images of these performers spring to mind and she flips the pages back to the point the cast have got to.

Palmer: Thank you Molly, you've been very helpful. Could you send Paul in please.

(Molly exits. Palmer paces the stage, deep in thought. Paul and Wendy enter)

Paul: It's like having to wait outside the headmaster's study. I'm being treated like a naughty schoolboy in my own house.

Palmer: I'm sorry you feel like that, but we are trying to discover your mother's murderer. And I did actually want to speak to you each alone.

Paul: Wendy and I don't have any secrets from each other, do we dear?

(*Wendy looks guilty*)

Palmer: Not from each other, well, perhaps, but what about from me?

Paul: Are you suggesting that I killed my mother? Why on earth should I do that?

Palmer: There seems to have been ill feeling about your mother making changes to her will, tell me about that.

Paul: No ill feeling from me, in fact if what she told us was really what she was going to do I stood to be better off. You should be asking Rita and Rosemary, especially Rita with that Patrick of hers always short of money and sponging off her.

Wendy: Paul, you shouldn't be trying to make the inspector suspicious, especially of your sister.

Paul: Why not? She's got more of a motive than either Rosemary or I.

Wendy: He doesn't really hate his sister that much, he's just upset by what's happened.

Palmer: Where were you when you heard the shot?

Paul: Oh I don't know, I was near the door to the dining room I think. We were all heading that way, well most of us. I think Rita was actually going upstairs, because she and Patrick were arguing with the rest of us about the will. I don't know where Rosemary and Stuart were. Wendy, had they already gone into the dining room? I bet you know where Stuart was.

Wendy: (*gives him a fierce look*) I don't think so, because we bumped into them about here when everyone started running to see what had happened.

Palmer: What about the servants?

Paul:	I don't waste my time keeping track of them. They should have been nearby because we were about to sit down to eat.
Palmer:	But your mother went into her study?
Wendy:	Obviously! That's where she was found.
Palmer:	Any idea why she might have gone in there instead of coming straight into the dining room?
Wendy:	Perhaps she was checking that none of us had been interfering with the will.
Paul:	You can't think that anyone would can you?
Wendy:	The other four weren't happy about it were they?
Paul:	Now who's pointing the finger Anyway someone shot her. That's all we can tell you.
Palmer:	And Molly found her?
Paul:	I think she must have been the first one to get there. She was certainly the one doing all the screaming. Annette came in and took her away.
Palmer:	Came in? Where from?
Wendy:	She'd been outside for something.

(*Palmer nods thoughtfully.*)

Mother had sent her to shut the front door.

Paul:	That was mother all over, we'd all been in and out of that door, what with bringing the cases in and parking the cars, and she just had to make the point that one of us might not have shut the door properly.
Palmer:	Your mother was particularly fussy?

Paul: She was a stickler for what she thought were the correct ways of doing things, and quite obsessed with security. She was very secretive. That's why there had been trouble when she thought Annette had been poking about in her desk. Mind you mother was probably right, she may well have been.

Palmer: So there's no possibility, with all her security, that anyone could have come in from outside and murdered her?

Paul: None at all.

Palmer: You realise that means the murderer was one of you.

"Miss Campbell, this is your call," Sally announces quietly.

You say Annette might have been looking in your mother's desk. What makes you say that?

Paul: The woman is downright nosy. She asks questions about the family and relationships all the time.

Wendy: She might just be trying to express an interest.

Paul: You didn't say that when she was prying into your fling with Stuart.

Palmer: Since you mention it, and I had heard rumours, tell me about that.

Paul: What's to tell. My dear wife had an affair with my brother in law.

Palmer: But it's over now?

(*Paul looks at Wendy, who looks away.*)

Paul: So I'm told.

Palmer: It's very important that you tell me eveything. (*a pause*) All right. Please don't leave the house I shall

> need to talk to you again. Perhaps you could send in your sister, er, Rosemary isn't it?

Wendy: I'll see if I can find her for you.

Chapter 5

Edward appears beside Sally. He has a tea-cloth in his hand and is drying one of the glasses that was used in act one. The show has some moments of activity for him, but like Sally he has become so used to the routine that he sometimes feels he is sleepwalking throughout the performance. Tonight he has kept so up to date with the cleaning up and re-setting ready for tomorrow's show that he can probably be out of the stage door mere seconds after the curtain comes down.

Glenda waits the act out in her room. She sometimes thinks she should take up a hobby, maybe knitting would be suitable for an aging actress with long periods of time on her hands. So far on this run she has read her way through a pile of rather trashy paperback romances, done an untold number of crosswords and sat and stared into space stroking the cat. In general she decides she prefers staring into space and stroking the cat, it takes mindless occcupations to the ultimate level. If she knitted she might have to concentrate on counting stitches. It seems to her entirely possible that, at her age, repeated counting is inviting her to fall asleep. Would it matter? She asks herself. The curtain call might be a bit ragged as a result but...

(*Rosemary enters slowly.*)

Palmer: Hello Mrs Dunford, just a few questions to help me sort this unfortunate matter out.

Rosemary: Is that what it is then, just an unfortunate matter?

Palmer: I'm sorry, I could have expressed myself better.

Rosemary: Yes you could have, but apology accepted.

Palmer: There are some things I need to know though. Were all of you on good terms before your mother was killed?

Rosemary: All families have disagreements. You must know that.

Palmer: What sort of disagreements were you all having?

Rosemary: I'm sure that you know that mummy was changing her will? The others weren't all too pleased.

Palmer: Which others particularly?

Rosemary: We'd been told about the new division of the estate. In a nutshell it gave Paul more and Rita and I less. There are a few fixed sums for the servants, but I don't really know if they went up or down. Oh and some to the church too. Mummy was having her solicitor in this morning to sign the new document. Clearly she didn't get to do that, so I suppose the old will still stands.

Palmer: So your mother's murder has worked to you and your sister's advantages?

Rosemary: What a horrid cruel way of looking at it.

Palmer: Mrs Dunford, I work in a horrid cruel business. There is no such thing as a kind murder, That's why I sometimes have to be horrid and cruel with my questions. You and your sister benefit financially from the situation. I would be foolish not to consider you among the suspects. Do you think your brother had influenced your mother to change her will?

Rosemary: Paul? Well I suppose he'd be better off, but ...

Palmer: Was there any reason why he might want you and your sister to be worse off? I want you to be honest.

Rosemary: That's an odd way round of looking at it. He doesn't like Patrick very much I suppose. Actually I don't think any of us do.

Palmer: Your sister's boyfriend? Any particular reason?

Rosemary: He's a bit of a gambler, and we all think he sponges off Rita all the while, but that's her business isn't it, if she choses to pay off his debts. You know what they say you can't chose your relatives, but sadly you also can't chose your in laws.

Palmer: And what about your husband?

Rosemary: What about Stuart?

Palmer: Is everything sunshine and light on the home front?

Rosemary: I don't know what you mean!

Palmer: I've heard that he 'strayed'.

Rosemary: Maybe, a bit.

Palmer: I heard that he strayed with Paul's wife.

Rosemary: Well if you knew that why did you need to ask?

Palmer: I wanted to see if you would tell me yourself. I need to know what people's reactions are. It tells me a lot that you had to have it dragged out of you.

Rosemary: All it tells you is that this family doesn't go around inviting gossip, airing its dirty linen. There are certain things that are private. To save you the trouble of asking your next questions, did Stuart and I have rows about it? Yes. Of course we did. Did Paul and Wendy fall out over it? I should think so, wouldn't you? What else would you like to know?

"Miss Fanthorpe, this is your call," Sally leans into the desk and gives the routine page.

Palmer: I think I need to talk to Mrs Burke.

Rosemary: *(after a hesitation)* Wendy?

Palmer: Of course, will you find her and send her in. Who did you think I meant?

Rosemary: Yesterday that would have meant mother, I haven't got used to Wendy becoming the head of the family, or at least her and Paul.

(*Palmer watches her leave suspiciously.*)

Sally shifts on her chair, lifts her arms above her head and stretches. Doing so knocks her headphones a little askew and she straightens them, realising from the noise down her earphones that the mic has been turned on since the last time she cued electrics right back at the start of the act. She says "Sorry for the noise chaps," to the operators, "Hope I didn't wake you up."

She hopes she hasn't been broadcasting any conversations. She can't remember having talked to anyone since the interval. Perhaps it's lucky Adrian wasn't saying anything suggestive tonight. She doesn't think the mic has been on that long, but you never know.

One of the control room crew says, "No, but we were getting a bit fed up with your snoring." It's an unusual bit of levity from the resident staff. She calls him a cheeky bugger and switches the mic off.

Palmer:	I'm glad to be able to speak to you alone, sometimes people are a bit inhibited when they are with others... I gather you can't think of anyone who would have wanted to kill your mother in law?
Wendy:	Oh yes, all the staff and most of the rest of the family I should imagine.
Palmer:	Can you give me any reasons?
Wendy:	How would you like to work for her? Oh I suppose you never met her. She was a controlling tyrant. She wanted everything done her way, the 'proper' way, and she was never satisfied, nothing was ever good enough.
Palmer:	Did she criticise you?

Wendy: From the moment I met Paul. I was never really suitable for him. She tried very hard to stop us getting married. No-one was ever going to be good enough for her precious Paul.

Palmer: And you think the others suffered in the same way and would want to kill her?

Wendy: A bit. Perhaps not enough to murder her, but they would all want to stop her signing the new will I imagine.

Palmer: You stood to be better off under the new will, so I understand. Were you and your husband alone in being eager to see her sign?

Wendy: Paul probably was. And I suppose you are right, I would be financially better off, through Paul, when she eventually died under what she said the new terms were. That didn't make me any more keen to see her die than I already was.

Palmer: Perhaps I should revise my view then; you and your husband are the only people in the house who are sorry she is dead.

Wendy: I didn't say I was sorry.

Palmer: Can we talk about Stuart Dunford?

Wendy: He didn't kill her.

Palmer: You seem very sure, how do you know?

Wendy: I.. I just know.

Palmer: May I assume that you were with Mr Dunford when you heard the shot then?

Wendy: Just for a few moments.

Palmer: And that was actually when the shot was fired, or just before?

Wendy: A little bit before, but Stuart couldn't have done it. Why would he?

Sally calls the cast for the denouement scene. In pairs or singly they all enter until everyone except Glenda is on stage. Adrian powers his way through his interrogations. He has the bulk of the script for this part of the show and dominates the stage. This is the long scene which justifies his star billing. She has to admit that he carries it very well. She is privately impressed by the actor's success at learning the pages of script he has to deliver. Much of his part is written as a long complex explanatory soliloquy, so he doesn't have the crutch of other actors' lines to help his memory. She knows that, despite daily repetition which means she knows the lines as well as anyone, she occasionally gets sort of mental blanks where she can't recall whether certain scenes have been played yet. It's probably due to not paying full attention. Auto-pilot she tells herself again. Familiarity has made her ignore the individual performances much of the time, but tonight she listens as Adrian unravels the plot for the audience. She suspects that many of the audience will have guessed the guilty party for themselves despite the slight plot twist.

Palmer: Perhaps we could start with you Miss Burke. What is your relationship with Patrick Fathers?

Rita: He's my boyfriend.

Palmer: Just that then, you aren't engaged?

(*Rita shakes her head*)

You see it's been suggested that your finance has gambling debts.

Rita: Maybe. Who 'suggested' that? Sometimes he does. What has it got to do with mummy's murder?

Palmer: Perhaps nothing, perhaps everything. You are short of

	money aren't you?
Rita:	A bit.
Palmer:	I think you were banking on what you would inherit when your mother died. I think that she told everyone she was going to change her will, and the new terms cut the amount you would receive. I think you killed her before she could sign the new will so as to protect your expected inheritance.
Rita:	That's not true!
Palmer:	Not true that the new will would have reduced your share of the estate, or not true that you killed her?
Rita:	I didn't kill her!
Palmer:	But you will admit that if she had changed her will you would have been worse off?
Rita:	I was going to talk to her after dinner. Make her see sense.
Palmer:	Let's talk about the gun.
Rita:	That old thing! I didn't even know it would fire.
Palmer:	Until you pulled the trigger?
Rita:	I never pulled the trigger. I didn't even know where it was till we all rushed in and it was lying there.
Palmer:	But you and your brother and sister used to play with it when you were children?
Rita:	Yes, but I didn't know where it was now, and I wouldn't have expected it to be loaded if I had.
Palmer:	Was it a surprise when it went off then? Did you threaten your mother with it, not knowing it was loaded?

Rita: I never touched it!

Palmer: Our fingerprint people say differently.

Rita: Well I might have picked it up when we all ran in. It was just lying there and mother was dead.

Palmer: Can you explain to me why you would pick the gun up then?

Rita: Just.. because. I don't know.

Palmer: Let me tell you what I think happened. I think you knew that your mother wasn't going to string along with your request for extra money. I think she knew where any extra money would go to, and she didn't like Patrick very much. I think that you guessed that the only way to ensure you got a big enough share was to force her to change her mind about the new will. You were desperate, so you went in with the gun and tried to force her. Whether you intended to carry out your threat we'll never know but somehow, either on purpose, or maybe by accident, you pulled the trigger and the gun went off. Am I right?

Rita: No! Nothing like that happened.

Palmer: But you were desperate for the money weren't you?

Rita: Patrick really needs it, he owes... well he owes some very nasty people.

Palmer: So you thought you'd help him, or rather you'd get the larger proportional share of the estate quicker.

Rita: It wasn't like that at all!

Palmer: What was it like then?

Sally is killing time by writing blank show report sheets ready for the next week. She writes the show, the date and 'time up' for each day. She feels it is like writing lines at school. 'I must not get bored with the show. I must not get bored with the show. I must not get bored...' Still at least once this task is done for the coming performances she will be able to amuse herself some other way. A crossword perhaps. She wonders if she could get away with a small portable television and some headphones. No, she disciplines herself, it would be most unprofessional. She knows of DSMs who have played chess with lighting operators using a set at each end of talk-back, but her contact with the venue's operators is so formal and tenuous that she doesn't really know how to suggest such an arrangement. She doesn't even know if either of the operators play chess.

She finishes the week's worth of pages and considers whether she dare fill in the time up, interval times and time down on the sheets in advance. It is so extremely unlikely that there will be any variation that she is sure she could get away with it. Is the entertainment industry the only one that delivers to such a precise timescale, she wonders. The rise of the curtain at the start of a show is more predictable than any railway timetable, than any delivery, than the repair man arriving.

Adrian is starting to explain his deduction.

Palmer: Mrs Morgan-Burke seems to have been quite an unpopular woman. Several of you had plausible valid reasons for wanting her dead. And that made it more difficult to sort out which of you actually killed her. For a while I wondered if you had all got together to murder her. In general terms it is easier for a group of people to murder an individual, because they can cover for each other. In an enclosed situation like this, all gathered in one house, it probably only needs a single bend of the truth to provide an alibi for everyone.
In this case it was unlikely. Partly because the servants were so closely involved with what happened, and partly because the family had some fairly fierce disagreements with each other so far as I can make out.
I did wonder if those disagreements were a

smokescreen, a deception, to mislead me. In some cases people were reluctant to admit to family disputes and that made me even more suspicious, because being, or appearing to be, unwilling to tell the police something is a way of making us more likely to accept it.

Paul: Perhaps we don't like outsiders snooping into our business.

Palmer: I'm afraid, Mr Burke, that, when a murder is committed, your business becomes public property.

Paul: It's bad enough that the local gossip mill will be working overtime, but do we have to have the servants here for this?

Palmer: All will become clear. As I said, this case involved everyone at some level.
I'm sure none of you will be too upset by things that may be revealed here tonight.
I have discovered that the murder weapon was not only kept casually in a drawer, but that it was well known to all of you that it was here. I'm told that it was even a plaything when you were children. Molly would quite likely have come across it when doing housework, and Annette almost certainly did when she opened your mother's desk. We know that Mrs Morgan-Burke saw Annette open her desk, there was some fuss about it I gather, so both the servants knew that the gun existed and where it was kept.

Rosemary: Are you saying it was one of them then?

Palmer: Please hear me out.
I had to ask myself, given the means, who among you had the motive?
It all seemed to relate to the will. Your mother had made no secret of her intention to change the terms, and had quite openly told you that the new will was to be signed almost immediately. She even told you the general facts about the new will, albeit reluctantly I

understand.

In essence two of the family stood to be a bit better off, and the remaining four a bit worse off in cash terms if Mrs Morgan-Burke were to sign the new document.

Paul: But we didn't know what she'd decided about the servants. She just said that they were getting lump sums. But she might have told them individually, so they could have had just as much motive.

Palmer: True. But Molly found the body.

Stuart: Or she killed Eleanor and then screamed.

Palmer: Just for the moment let's get back to the family.

Paul: Wendy and I had a vested interest in the new will getting signed, so that counts us out.

Palmer: Not entirely. I understand that you, Wendy and you, Stuart had an affair recently...

Paul: It might still be going on.

Palmer: The point is that if either of your spouses had said they were considering divorce you would both benefit from inheritances coming though sooner rather than later, whatever the division of the estate turned out to be.

Rosemary: I notice you haven't mentioned Rita.

Palmer: But I haven't forgotten her either. You see from what I can make out Rita needs the money much more than any of the rest of you. Actually it's Patrick who needs the money. I've asked around, and it seems that Patrick has made a bad mistake by getting into debt. Worse he has got into debt with some rather tough types. They are well known to us in the force, and, though we have never been able to make any accusations stick we are pretty sure that their debt collection techniques are, shall we say, 'robust'. Patrick may well find himself very badly hurt if he can't raise the money he owes by whatever is the next deadline they have given him. Am I right?

Patrick: Yes, I need the money. Rita was going to try to persuade her mother to give us an advance to fend the lenders off. There's no chance of that now.

Palmer: You will have the inheritance though, or Rita will, at the old, higher share division. You must be relieved by that.

Patrick: Yes, No, We didn't kill her. Why would Rita kill her mother?

Palmer: To save your skin, of course.

Chapter 6

Sally realises again that she hasn't been turning the pages for a while, and begins flipping through the script to catch up. She has been day-dreaming, wondering whether, in the few confused moments prior to the shot, Tessa and Gregory's characters have really had any amount of time together away from the rest of the company as the script says. She is sure the blocking hasn't picked up on this line and shown them together but distanced from the crowd at that point. As the weeks have dragged on she has spotted increasing numbers of instances where the direction has failed to reflect the scripted lines very well.

Palmer: Sometimes the most conspicuous people are not the actual culprits.

Wendy: What do you mean?

Palmer: All through this we've been looking at the six of you, the children and spouses.. It's a loose description Mr Fathers.. 'partner' or 'boyfriend' if you prefer, because you all have perfectly good, mostly financial, reasons for wishing Mrs Morgan-Burke dead. But what if there were others who had similar axes to grind?
Mrs Morgan-Burke was not the easiest person to get along with from what I have been told. Her children only visited occasionally. What if the petty annoyances had built up and caused Molly or Annette to attack their employer?

Paul: Ah, now we're getting to it.

Molly: Oh, inspector, you don't really mean me do you? After all it was me who found her.

Palmer: It was, or it seemed to be, but was she alive when you first went in? How much annoyance had built up in the, what was it? twenty years that you have worked here.

Stuart: You've all known Molly for most of your lives, She

wouldn't kill your mother, would she?.

Wendy: I agree with Stuart, the idea is absurd.

Paul: Yes, you would agree with Stuart wouldn't you?

Wendy: Well I do agree with him, he's right!

Palmer: Tell us what you saw when you went in to the room, Molly.

Molly: It was horrible, she was lying there, and there was all that blood.

Palmer: So you called the others?

Molly: I just screamed.

Palmer: Do you remember who arrived first?

Molly: No. I think they all came together, pretty much.

Palmer: Perhaps you and Annette knew what you were going to get under the new will. Perhaps it wasn't as much as it had been in the old will. Perhaps you both thought that preventing it being signed was to your advantage. We know that there are members of the family who stood to be better off, and members of the family who might be getting a smaller slice of the cake. Did you two know how the revised bequests would change things for you?

Annette: We didn't know anything. Well I didn't, did you, Molly?

Molly: No, Mrs Morgan-Burke didn't tell me anything about it. I didn't realise that this was anything other than a family get together.

Palmer: Ah yes, about the family gathering. Not all the family it seems. Who among you knew about Mrs Morgan-Burke's other child?

Paul: What 'other child'?

Palmer: Apparently your mother had a fourth child at some point but it was sent for adoption straight after it was born. If that child is now grown up and has discovered its real parentage it would have a claim on the estate. I'm certain that Molly only let slip the secret by accident. For the missing child to be among you it could only be Patrick, unless someone is in an incestuous marriage. If it is Patrick that would explain Rita's reluctance to get engaged to him if she knew. Is it you Patrick?

Patrick: What an absurd suggestion.

Palmer: Then, alternatively, if the child has managed to work its way into the household it can only be Annette.

(*Palmer looks directly at Annette, who looks uncomfortable*)

Well?

Annette: Yes, yes, all right then. I found out about my parentage by chance. I thought if I could get into the house I would be able to find some sort of proof so I could claim my rightful share.

Paul: That's why you were forever asking about the family history and why you were poking about in mother's papers. Spying!

Annette: No, not spying, trying to find out about my family.

Paul: It's not your family. You were sent away. Mother never mentioned anything about you. She clearly didn't want you.

Annette: Obviously she didn't want me. Over the years I've come to the conclusion that I might not have been Mr Morgan-Burke's child. If I was someone else's it would explain why I was given away. You won't upset me by sneering and rejecting me, I've lived with the rejection for a long while. But now she is dead I will be claiming my share.

Palmer: Or maybe you won't.

Paul: We're not dividing mother's estate with a servant!

Palmer: Annette Russell, I advise you to be very careful what you say. It seems more than possible that you were responsible for the death of Mr Morgan-Burke, and if so you do realise that you will not inherit anything. You can't benefit from a crime.

Annette: I didn't kill her!

Palmer: You had the means, once you found the gun, abandoned in a drawer and mostly forgotten. You found some ammunition, or you got some from somewhere, and then you were ready to kill your employer. You had a motive, and this gathering for the will signing was a major advantage to you, because the more people in the house the easier it was to disguise what you were doing. There was your opportunity, and you took it. You shot Mrs Morgan-Burke while everyone else was away getting changed for dinner. Molly happening to come running and finding the body was another stroke of luck, because her hysterical screams gave you an excellent excuse to appear from wherever you had hidden after firing the gun and take her away. What more natural than for the housekeeper to try to comfort the maid after such a shock.
Now all you needed to do was wait until the estate was being dealt with before revealing your true identity.
I imagine you have all the necessary papers ready to be produced.

Annette: Yes I do, But you are quite wrong. I didn't kill anyone.

Palmer: You admit you have a claim to part of the estate. You

	admit that you have been working here under a false name waiting for the moment to reveal that you might be the late Mrs Morgan-Burke's daughter. Why didn't you tell everyone this when you first came to work here?
Annette:	I am her daughter. It's not a false name, the Russells adopted me as a baby, and I had to make sure I could prove the relationship before I said anything. Anyway I couldn't say anything at first because Mrs Morgan-Burke would have been annoyed, and in an embarrassing position when her secret was revealed..she might have sacked me to hush it up.
Palmer:	So you killed her to remove that problem.
Annette:	No.
Palmer:	And your need to prevent our victim from signing the new will was even greater than the family's because your presence would slice the cake into even more pieces, but if the new will gave a specific value bequest to you in your guise as Annette Russell you wouldn't be allowed a proportional share as well.
Annette:	I don't know about the legal ins and outs, but I didn't kill her.
Palmer:	Annette Russell I am arresting you for the murder of....

As every night there is a general hubub as Adrian recites the caution.

Annette:	All right, I'll admit I'm the missing child. I'll admit....
Palmer:	I must warn you that you are under caution!
Annette:	Will admit that I got myself a job here because I was trying to trace my parentage. You know all this, but it doesn't make me guilty of killing my mother!
Molly:	Annette couldn't have done it anyway.

Palmer: What do you mean? What have you not told me?

Molly: When we heard the shot Annette and I were both in the kitchen, we were getting dinner ready, remember, it just so happened I was nearest to the door and ran out to see what was going on first.

Palmer: But Mrs Morgan Burke sent Annette outside.

Annette: To check the door was locked, yes, but I came back in by the kitchen door and got on with preparing dinner.

Molly: So you see it couldn't have been her.

Paul: I think that leaves you back at square one, inspector.

(*there is a confused babble as everyone starts to speak at once. Rita doesn't join in and is staring down at the floor*)

Rita: (*quietly*) I did it.

(*The confession goes unheard in the rowdiness*)

Rita: (*more forcefully*) I did it.

(*all react to this announcement.*)

Palmer: It's a very serious matter, wasting police time by fraudulent claims. Think carefully before you say anything else.

Rita: It's not a frudulent claim. You were quite right, Patrick needs the money to buy off the loan sharks. I tried to get mother to give us some sort of advance, but... well you know what she could be like. She wouldn't have any of it, in fact she threatened to write me out of her will completely.

Palmer: You realise that Patrick won't get any of the money now you've confessed, don't you?

Rita: There wasn't going to be enough any more once Annette popped up wanting to grab a share... Oh I don't blame her, she probably is entitled to some, after mother rejected her and sent her away, but my share was only just enough before, So I'm sorry Patrick, you're on your own!

Sally puts lighting and sound on standby for the end of the show. Just a few more lines of script to go. She says, "Miss Littlewood, this is your call for the curtain call," into the microphone. Everyone else is already on stage. David has appeared by the tab rope. She gives him a nod of acknowledgement.. 'stand by' is tacitly assumed through long habit.

Chapter 7

The show is over once again. The tabs are in, muffling the audience applause for the moment, as the cast reposition themselves for the curtain call. There is an urgency about this, it is not just that the curtain must rise again before the audience's clapping begins to wane, but also the evening's work is now done. Another performance concluded. The players' minds are turning to getting out of costume and going home.

The cast forms a line just behind the house curtain. They are holding hands as they face the audience, it makes it easier to synchronise bowing together. Glenda in the centre squeezes the hands of Steven and Adrian either side of her and they relay the pressure along the line each way to the rest.

David, following Sally's 'up' and 'down' gestures with no more than half an eye, flies the tabs out and in for curtain calls. Each night is the same, though the occasional Saturday night audience may, rarely, be enthusiastic enough to be allowed an additional bow. This is not the case tonight, and the cast line breaks up once the bows are over as the actors turn away and return to their dressing rooms. Long habit means they hardly talk to each other as they go off the stage. Even the routine comments about the audience, 'good house', or 'stodgy audience', have mostly fallen by the wayside as the run has got longer. Rarely, but not tonight, an individual member of the audience in the front couple of rows, the only seats really visible to the cast against the glare of the stage lights, may be conspicuous enough to arouse a comment among the performers, but mostly the show ends, just as it does tonight, with a disappointingly flat feeling backstage.

David pushes the brake down firmly on the tab rope as Sally writes the 'time down' in the show log.

The lighting and sound operators would be first out of the stage door after the performance if they didn't have to wait till the last tail-ender has left the auditorium. From the control room window they can see three small knots of people in the theatre. One is a couple near the front in about D row, who are fidgeting about and looking under seats, obviously having lost something. An usherette appears beside them, some conversation takes place and then there is more tipping up of seats before the elderly man is handed a flat cap that has evidently slipped down the back of his chair. They leave. Almost exactly in the centre of the stalls a cluster of similarly elderly people are deep in discussion, seemingly making no move toward the exits, though they have at least stood up. The third slow leavers are a young couple who are still seated and seem intent on finishing their box of chocolates before moving off.

Douglas has stood in his foyer watching the slow departure of the audience. The scrums around the doors to the toilets have gradually dwindled and the stairways are clear again of members of the public feeling their way down, clinging carefully to the brass bannisters in the crush. The sales staff are jumping the gun a bit by starting to pack up and close down their outlets while potential customers are still in the building, but he doesn't really blame them. At this time of night they all want to move the tail enders out into the street so they can shut and chain the building's doors. It is not a show that sells any merchandise, and programme sales have taken place before the start, or in very few cases in the interval. It would be exceptional for a customer to be trying to buy anything as they leave, though he keeps the staff at their posts in case.

The sound operator slowly fades down the play-out music and switches off the system. There is a faint 'pop' from the PA as the last power supply shuts down. The tail enders are finally starting to move. The lighting operator stands with one hand on the switch for the cleaning lights. The final customers vanish from view. After a few moments an usherette looks up at the control room and waves 'all clear' to him. He flicks a switch and the auditorium instantly feels cold and austere in the working lights for the house staff to do the basic litter pick-up. He fades out the decorative houselights and kills the rosy glow of tab-warmers. The two operators leave together, going backstage via one of the pass doors and pausing briefly to isolate the lighting and stage power at the switch room near the stage door. They say goodnight to Reg as they go out amid brief 'see you tomorrow's.

Reg is standing now in the doorway of his hutch, politely, almost subserviently, wishing 'good night' to each member of the cast and crew in turn. They hand him dressing room keys as they leave.

Edward and Sally are very prompt tonight, leaving ahead of the cast, and together. He doesn't think that there is anything going on between them, though something tells him that Edward would like there to be, so it must be just one of those co-incidences.

Next comes Alan, "Goodnight Mr. Hattersley," and then Beth, who fumbles handing the key to him because she is also clutching an envelope. The letter has been opened, and as she swops it to her other hand to free the key he can see the paper is printed with the blue and white NHS logo. He says "Goodnight Miss Johnstone. Thank you," as the keys are put into his palm.

Julia is loitering in the lobby. Reg wonders if she is really waiting for Steven Truss this time. He hasn't failed to notice Steven's repeated attempts to leave with her over the past weeks.

Anne sweeps through the lobby, looking neither left nor right and ignoring Reg's "Goodnight Miss Birkett." He can tell she is in a mood again. This is the case more often than not. He watches her back as she slams though the narrow double doors wrapping her coat more firmly around her shoulders. He is sure that there is a marital rift between the Birketts, but he cannot be certain why. This company has not acquired the habit of passing its internal gossip to him as a matter of course, and he is no better informed than anyone else in the building.

Jessica and Gregory leave together, Gregory is solicitously holding her arm, which makes her appear to be a frail old lady.

"Goodnight Miss Campbell, Mr. Bradford." Gregory starts to say goodnight to Reg, but adopting the role of the grande-dame Jessica over-rides his words with, "Goodnight Reg. Thank you so much. See you tomorrow." as if he had performed some memorable service for her, rather than just handing her dressing room key and post over each day as she came in.

They have hardly left the building before Steven appears and goes straight over to Julia, taking her by the hand and tossing his room key casually to Reg, who catches it in mid flight, saying, "Goodnight Mr. Truss," and slightly pointedly, "Miss Varley." "Thanks Reg," floats back over Steven's shoulder and they too are gone.

'I was right then' Reg thinks, as Adrian hands him his key. "Goodnight Mr Birkett." He wonders whether to tell the actor that his wife has left before him, but is sure that the man already knows that, even if they are not in the same dressing room.

There is a pause, during which Reg carefully hangs the keys back on their respective hooks. Rosencrantz has comandeered the single chair and is curled up on the worn seat cushion. He doesn't move the cat aside. He looks at his watch. The night watchman is due any moment. He tidies the little office while he waits, stacking the used tabloid newspaper and a copy of 'The Stage' to one side for his colleague to read overnight, moving the tea and coffee-making things about on the tray which they and the kettle live on and squaring up the envelopes in the pigeon holes. He waits. Glenda is always last.

When she does arrive it is as if she expects a crowd of autograph hunters; and a limo to sweep her away. If Jessica was playing the big star as she left Glenda really is it. One night, Reg thinks, they will both be leaving at exactly the same time, and sparks are certain to fly. He is sure that both women are more than capable of sharp barbed comments if necess.ary. He anticipates the possibility as a relief from the routine

He can see that despite having taken the longest and being last Glenda has failed to remove all traces of make-up and no-one in the street would have the slightest difficulty in categorising her as 'actress'. Unless they thought... No. Reg stops short of that unkind idea.

"Goodnight Miss Littlewood."

"Thank you Reg, Goodnight to you," The key is offered dangling from the fingers of an outstretched hand. Reg shrewdly allows her to drop it into his palm, recognising that she is playing a part, a part that would not have been out of place in a nineteen-fifties film. The condescending politeness of the stars of that era has gradually given way to a more abrupt, demanding, attitude during his time as a doorman. He misses the old fashioned courtesies, but accepts that they will not return.

The cast are all gone, and he shuts and locks one half of the narrow double doors that form the barrier between the fantasy world inside the building and the grey reality of real life. The night-watchman slips inside through the shrinking gap as Reg does this.

Later Steven and Julia are on the tube. It has been a pleasant meal. True to form Steven has been amusing, the old fashioned word might be 'witty', and Julia sits beside him, warm, well fed and just a little tipsy from the wine with their meal. She is contented enough to ignore the empty drinks can rolling on the curved ribbed carriage floor nearby, and its irregular rattle as bends in the track make it shift from one side of the aisle to the other. They are on the sideways facing seats and she can see their own reflections in the window opposite, overlaying the grey blur of mysterious cables looping hypnotically in a succession of swoops along the tunnel wall, lit by the harsh glare of the carriage's interior, as the train rattles its late night way toward her flat. The carriage is almost empty and the only other occupants, both men, far away down the car, are staring passively at empty space.

Lights, and slowing to a halt with the familiar red, white and blue roundel bearing a station name on the curved wall that seems just inches from the window becoming partially obscured by the frame of the sliding door now opening opposite her. 'Three more stops', she thinks, reading the name plate, and begins to wonder what will happen then, though deep down she knows exactly how the rest of the evening is going to play out. She isn't really eager or enthusiastic. Willing, maybe. More like resigned. He's pleasant, amusing, he will be company, but he's not really her ideal fanciable man, however she's tired and woozy, 'Woozy and boozy!' she thinks, and smiles to herself, expanding this to 'I'm a woozy, boozy, floozy'. She rests her head on his shoulder more in resignation and friendship than anticipation. Steven is a little surprised, though pleased. He tightens the arm that is around her shoulder and she doesn't protest. He is led to believe his long slow wooing of the girl has worked.

Now the train is going round a sweeping curve. The wheels screech against the rails and the noise is unpleasant in the carriages. Julia knows this noise, this is her stop. She raises herself, stands, holding the chrome upright pole and takes a pace to the doors exactly as they part for her to step down onto the platform, with the practiced but unconscious skill of the regular tube user at their home stop. On the platform she looks back over her shoulder, half wondering if he will follow her. He does, and the doors slide shut behind him, commiting him to this station as she leads the way to the escalators.

At her bed-sit she makes them coffee, but it is eventually left abandoned as the inevitable end of the evening happens.

In the morning Julia wakes to discover that her fellow actor has gone. Vanishing without a farewell, it gives her a feeling of having been used. She spends the day on housekeeping, and, finding she has an urge to do so, washing all the bedding. The rumble of the machine is followed by the slow churning of the drier. She has to have the kitchen window open because of the steam and she eats her lunch to a background of these domestic appliances and the noise of the London street below. She doesn't find this familiar or comforting, she can hardly remember the last time she had these windows open. The tiny balcony off her living room normally offers enough space for a short washing line which can cope with all her drying needs. Today she has washed too much and the weather is damp and drizzly. She finds herself forced to use the tumble drier.

In another flat Anne and Adrian are trying to ignore each other. Their joint home is not really big enough for this to work and despite living independent lives they find themselves in the same room more often than Anne wishes. They have each had their own bedroom for a long time but she knows that he stayed out all night, returning in the mid morning just as she was drinking her coffee. She is under no illusions, certain that once again he has been in another woman's bed. She has her suspicions about who he was with this time, another page from his address book perhaps, and feels sorry for the girl, whoever she is, rather than jealous of , or angry at, her. She is angry with him though. She is cross with herself for succumbing to his racy charm and marrying him. Perhaps women always think that they will be the one to change the behaviour of the man. She is livid with him about the address book. Was last night one of those girls, or, she fears, perhaps Sally or Julia? They are the only two in this production in Adrian's usual target age range. She has experienced him having flings with company members working on the same show as her before and knows the backstage tensions that result when he dumps them, as he always does. Is that what will happen this time? She thinks so. If his conquest was one of those two it has taken him a long while. He usually moves faster than that with these one night stands. She knows that he took the car last night, but that tells her nothing about where he went and with whom. She doesn't know where either of the girls on the show live. After nearly a year they must have flats within reasonable striking distance of the theatre, but the late night busses and the underground make any guess of distance or direction impossible. She remembers some fragmented chatter during rehearsals about what accomodation people had arranged, and recalls that some of the cast said they already had London flats, but the details escape her now.

She has commandeered the Birkett's flat's small lounge, so Adrian is ensconced in the kitchen as they avoid each other. She seems relaxed in an armchair with the newspaper open on her lap, but internally she is seething. It is uncomfortable and disturbing to constantly be in a state of anger and annoyance with no immediate alleviation for the emotion in sight. Over and over again she finds her mind wandering to the guns on the props table, so tempting. She can remember the smooth cold weight of the one she has picked up and the enticing balance of it in her grip. How strange that something designed to kill should have such a tempting tactile design. It might be worth the risk just to hold the thing with a purpose in mind, to allow it to fulfil the role it was built for.

She would have to plan it well. She would need some live ammunition. She has no intention of being detected and going to prison, but he does so deserve it, and she can always dream.

Adrian is sitting at the kitchen table. He has his book of names in front of him, but it is closed. Last night's drive had been a long one, taking him right down to the coast and to a dark lonely graveyard. Using the torch from the car he had found the girl's grave with its forlorn stone... 'to the memory of Naomi Johnstone'. Funny how his memory of the funeral had played tricks with him. His recollection of where he had stood watching them bury Bunny turned out to be quite inaccurate. He had had to search for a long time before he found the right headstone. Even in the dark he had been able to see the unkempt grass and weeds. Bunny's family had clearly stopped tending the grave. Maybe, very possibly, her parents are now dead. Presumably the little sister has moved away from the area. Adrian had lingered for a long while plucking at the long grass by hand and pulling up the worst of the weeds, clearing away in front of the headstone so the wording is legible once more.

Now back in the flat, even with the atmosphere that exists between him and Anne, he has shaken off the morbid curiosity that caused the night time drive. He feels weary and grubby from being up all night, but somehow relieved at the evidence that no-one is actively mourning Bunny any longer. Clearly she has been forgotten by the world and no-one any longer cares. Perhaps he himself cared enough last night to make the pilgrimage, but that is over now and he need never think about it again.

Chapter 8

Friday evening

Reg greets the crew, and then the cast, back into the theatre. The residents either give him a cursory nod as they pass, or stop for a brief word about the weather. The crew who work for the show are more inclined to chat, for, although the length of the run so far has made them almost honoury members of the building's staff they still feel that they should be thanking him for his services. He is not one of their number. He has not gone through the weeks of rehearsal and now repeated performances. He is outside their specific group but theatre produces a clannish companionship alongside the desperate desire to talk to real people.

First of the performers, and even beating some of the crew into the venue, he is unsurprised to see, is Glenda. First in, last out has become the normal routine. She is old school. Thorough in her preparations, which are heavy enough for her to need extra time at the end to clean her make-up off. Anyway, he decides, she is older and therefore probably slower. It doesn't occur to him that she is also alone and lonely and that even the small chance of a conversation with another cast or crew member would be welcome.

He hands her the dressing room key, and she accepts it, along with a few envelopes which are possibly fan mail, giving him an over-gracious smile and thank-you. Julia Varley follows close on the older actress' heels. Reg thinks that she seems rather pensive and wonders if something has upset her. Perhaps her date with Steven last night did not go well. He had rather expected them to re-appear together this evening. He could hardly have watched the comings and goings through this door for as long as he has without being conscious of the pairings, and Julia and Steven were the most conspicuous last night. Surprise comes when the Birketts arrive together. Reg was sure that that couple's rift had reached the point where they were leading completely unconnected lives, in fact he has detected what seems to be outright hatred on the part of Anne for her husband on some occasions.

Tessa Fanthorpe has trouble crossing the road outside the theatre. She stands on the edge of the pavement as lines of vehicles crawl past in both directions in an unbroken stream, tyres hissing on the wet road surface. She studies the front of the theatre as she waits. Its brickwork is verging on black from the city grime which has lodged into every crevice in the ornate Victorian building. The public front doors, still firmly shut at this time, have very fancy brass handles polished, at least on the raised portions of their decorative shapes, by the constant handling of arriving and departing audiences. Through the etched glass panels with their scolling foliage designs, the foyer is still dark, though shadowy figures are moving about inside stocking the bars and merchandising outlets. Above a huge white billboard announces 'All Invited To A Murder' in red block capitals. To either side giant photgraphs of Glenda and Adrian flank smaller boards, each with a list of the cast names. Small signs stick outward from the frontage dangling over the pavement with more red lettering. At this angle she can just read 'Outstanding, Evening Standard' through the drizzle. Cynically she wonders if the original review actually said 'this show is not outstanding'. She guesses she has been with the play too long and become bored with it. Long runs can become too much like factory production lines and this tendency is markedly the case with the straight play format.

A figure joins her on the kerb. It is Beth, also attempting to cross the road. They nod to each other. When the wait has become too long not to speak Tessa says, "This doesn't get any better does it?"

Cars, lorries and buses swish past in both directions, headlights probing the early evening semi-darkness. The two actresses clutch at their coats as the slipstream of an articulated lorry blasts at them.

"Have you ever thought that we are responsible for some of this?" Beth says, gesturing at the rush hour traffic as it grinds its way remorselesly through the city's streets.

"Not me. I don't even drive," Tessa replies, "let alone a lorry... or a bus," she adds as one passes them.

"No? But you're causing some of it you know."

"I didn't cause it. Don't blame me," Tessa feels grumpy at the accusation.

Beth says, "Every night, and twice on Saturdays, we cause over a thousand people to head to this street to watch the show. Then about three hours later we turn them all out into the highways and byways again all at once. Every other show in town does the same. Certain to lead to traffic chaos. We probably shouldn't grumble if we can't cross the road."

Tessa has never really considered this aspect of her profession. Like most performers she is blissfully unaware of all the multiple elements that are dragged together to make the production happen night after night. She is conscious of how a show provides both entertainment to its audience and employment to a huge range of hidden workers. She does derive some small pride from that. She says:

"It's not exactly our fault."

"Everyone always says 'it's not my fault'. Some people should reap the consequences of their actions." There is more bitterness in Beth's words than might have been expected from the slight delay in crossing a road, however damp and miserable the capital's weather happened to be.

Tessa notices and thinks this is a rather harsh opinion. She is about to ask if Beth is suggesting doing away with live theatre and making everyone stay at home to watch tele, but a gap in the traffic and the coincidence of some sets of nearby traffic lights turning red allows the two actresses to make a precipitate dash across the road and the conversation is interrupted. They go down the side of the theatre to the stage door, where Reg greets them with keys, and a letter for Tessa.

"Nothing for you today I'm afraid," he tells Beth, "Still you can't have exciting mystery packages every day can you?"

She doesn't respond, her mind is still on the letter she has had earlier this week, and its consequences. She goes straight up to the dressing rooms.

Eventually he has handed over all the keys and post and given suitable polite greeting to each of the cast. The racing pages of the evening paper are calling, and he settles into his accustomed place.

Sally and Edward are setting up. The house tabs dangle six or eight foot from the stage floor as they give the set its daily sweep.

Out in the auditorium members of the house staff are going up and down rows and aisles checking. A very few of them look to the stage to see what is going on there. The scene is too familiar to them to arouse any curiosity. They have all seen the set.

Edward is pushing the wide broom in a systematic pattern to cover the area that they have exposed by flipping the edges of the carpet, that covers most of the stage, back. He stops at one point and picks up a stray object.

"Where the hell did that come from?" he asks Sally, holding a cartridge between finger and thumb for her inspection. She takes it from him and looks at it.

"Well it's a live one, so I didn't miss the bin throwing it away. I suppose I must have dropped it when I was loading. Odd though, I would have thought I'd have noticed." She balances the blank shell on the desk beside the prompt copy and returns to her preparations.

When the carpets are flipped back flat on the floor again and the furniture correctly re-positioned David appears and flies the tabs back to their 'in' dead, just touching the stage. He is wary around Sally tonight. He has spent a night of exaggerated frustration and fantasising since watching Adrian with the girl at the last performance, and doesn't really know what to do. Overnight he has considered approaching her with an outright declaration of his feelings, asking her out for a drink or a meal, or even grabbing her physically as Adrian seemed to do yesterday. As he is rather painfully shy he knows that he will do none of these things, and that knowledge feeds his pent up and frustrated anger against the actor for his easy and confident familiarity with the girl. 'If only..' he thinks.

Abruptly the preset lighting state comes on above them as they prepare. Sally looks at her watch, but it is too early for the half. The electrics boys are ahead of themselves tonight. She picks up her headphones and says 'hello', but as usual there is no reply from the room at the rear of the auditorium.

"Normal tea tonight then," says Edward.

Sally hushes him, "Don't let them hear you on the show relay, it's much more interesting when they don't know what to expect."

Momentarily they giggle like naughty children, turning away from the prompt desk microphones quite illogically, as the show relay mic is somewhere high above them in the centre of the stage.

David watches their relaxed chat, feeling sad at his inablity to join in naturally with the informal chatter.

Sally is slightly relieved that Beth hasn't come to find her to complain about last night's tea. Edward's game of Russian roulette with the brands is mildly amusing, but the actress' annoyance has sometimes been extreme. There is a hardness behind the woman's exterior that Sally dislikes. She thinks it is as though she is nursing a grievance. Maybe given some of the teas she's been given she has some justification.

Edward goes off and sets up the tea things, fills the kettle and gives it a preliminary boil so it will take less time when the actual brewing occurs.

Sally continues her pre-show checks. The stage is set, everything is in its proper place for the top of the show. Personal props are all there.

She fetches the guns, and reloads the one that she uses, putting the blank shell that Edward swept up into the chamber and making sure it is ready to fire. She fails to notice a fractional difference in the colour of the shell in the spare gun. It is hardly visible anyway with the cylinder closed, and knowing she hasn't used it she doesn't bother to check that weapon. In the dim working lights of the wings the way the edge of the brass cartridge in the spare glints differently from its twin is very subtle.

On the floor below, in the lobby by Reg's hutch, Tessa is standing in the corner, under the grey curved metal and plastic dome that surmounts the payphone. She doesn't ring her mother nearly as often as she should. She never did. She remembers that her time at acting school was punctuated by repeated letters, and more embarassingly post cards, for everyone in the house could read those, from her mother, all saying 'are you all right? I haven't heard from you for several days'. As a grown-up, appearing in a London show, who has spent most of her life avoiding contact with an estranged matriarch, she is only pushed to making a duty call every week or two. She huddles into the sound-deadened space as she dials. Ringing tone, and eventually her mother's voice, querrelous and suspicious. Tessa says 'hello' studying the regular perforations on the inside of the dome. Some are enlarged and distorted where idle users have poked them while phoning. The blue smears around the damaged holes betray the vandals as having attacked the soft perforated card lining with the point of a biro. The same, or other, biros have written unidentified phone numbers on the surfaces.

She knows that in theory the dome stops people from outside from hearing her conversation, just as it is supposed to quieten the noise from the surrounding area. She also knows it doesn't work. On the other side of the lobby she can see Reg behind his desk, and she knows he can hear everything.

"Yes mother, yes its me... no nothing's wrong I just thought I'd ring you." She turns so she is facing directly away from Reg. She thinks how stupid it is to be bothered about him hearing her talking to her mother but somehow phoning home makes her believe that people listening in are comparing her to an errant schoolgirl. In truth there are similarities with boarding school; the completely separate life from the rest of the family, and this occasional duty call to prove she is still alive and well.

"No mother, the show is fine... No they haven't sacked me." She remembers how her mother can turn the simplest statement into some imagined disaster. "Nothing to report." She gives up and confesses, "Actually its rather boring. Same old, same old. Day after day... No really, it would be nice if something different did happen... Well I don't know what, maybe I could try playing it with an Irish accent for a change... Well of course they'd be cross if I did... No mother I promise I won't."

Reg grins to himself, reassured that the cast are sticking to their routine. Tessa makes one of these calls to her mother every so often. As an involuntary eavesdropper to the cast phone calls he can form imagined images of the invisible families at the other end of the lines. In the case of Tessa's mother he has deduced how the woman repeatedly twists every comment to the worst possible scenario. The actress seems to have to follow any piece of news she announces with a reassurance that all is well. He feels sorry for Tessa deducing she finds the calls a trial.

On stage Sally checks the clock, though she knows she has reset the hands.

She looks at her watch, it is exactly five to seven, and speaks into the microphone, pressing the square red button below it in a casual way from long familiarity.

"Good evening ladies and gentlemen, this is your half hour call. Half an hour please. Thank you."

She writes the date, and 'Time up' ready on the stage manager's report sheet. The run is so routine that the sheets rarely show anything other than timings, and those vary by mere seconds each performance. She longs to have something, almost anything to report.

At the phone Tessa tells her mother, "I'll have to go, that's the half... The half hour call mother... for the start of the show... yes... yes I must go, goodbye..." eventually she hangs up, sees Reg looking and shrugs, saying "Mothers!" as she goes toward the dressing rooms. He smiles sympathetically as she turns away from him to make her way our of the lobby and up to the dressing rooms.

"Where's Rosencrantz tonight?" Sally asks Edward when he comes back.

"Haven't seen him today, so he's probably with Reg," Edward tells her.

"He doesn't love you any more,"

"He 'loves' anyone who pays attention to him, and preferably feeds him," Edward assures her.

The play-in music starts a bit belatedly and can just be discerned on-stage.

In the foyer the front of house staff light up the entrances, open the doors and the public begin to trickle in. Douglas is standing on the first floor landing tonight, from where he can supervise the foyer below and the entrances to the circle. As always his black suit and bow tie are immaculate. He is wearing his habitual air of aloof superiority. It is a typical house, with a slightly older demographic than most London shows achieve. Among the audience the early arrivers are directed to their seats and then spend much of their time standing up, pushing back against the tipped up seat, to allow later patrons to squeeze past them along the row. There are murmured 'sorries' and 'thank-yous' as this goes on all over the house. Programmes are rustled, pages turned, and cast biographies studied and commented on. There are some 'I remember seeing her in that' type statements where the reader spots a familiar show title in the biographical write-up for one of the company.

Backstage Jessica is smearing Leichner on her face thickly again. With a cursory knock Gregory is with her. He stands behind her, looking at her reflection in the mirror. They say hello to each other but there is no conversation. Idly he picks up a make-up stick from the table and plays with it. For once Jessica's irritation boils over;

"Oh do stop fiddling with my make-up," she snaps at him.

Gregory is slightly taken aback. He steps away from her, says "OK. Sorry, See you on the green," and leaves. He is still holding the stick of greasepaint as he wanders to the stage. Sally has just given the latest call:

"Ladies and gentlemen this is your fifteen minute call. Quarter of an hour please. Thank you."

Gregory idles by the props table, drawn to the guns as everyone seems to be. He picks up the spare, holding it in the same hand as Jessica's make up. He realises this and tries to extract the make-up from his grip with his free hand without dropping the gun. The fat stick of number nine smears the trigger guard as he does so, but in the dim light of the wings no-one sees.

Sally turns to look at him and says, "Everything all right Greg?"

He nods, so she says, "Please don't fiddle with the props, they've been set."

This is the second time in a few minutes that he has been told not to 'fiddle' with things, he begins to get a feeling he is not wanted. He shrugs, betraying a listlessness that he had hardly been aware of, and, laying the gun down he wanders off to his own dressing room. Sally gets up from her desk and goes to pick up the spare gun and hang it by its cord on the hook. This disturbance of routine makes her study the props table again, but otherwise everything seems normal.

Edward comes and stands by Sally, picking short grey hairs from his stage black clothes.

"You found Rosencrantz then?" she guesses, looking him up and down.

"He was alseep on the shelves above the sink in the props room."

"Does he have to moult this much all the time?" she says, and starts helping Edward to rid himself of the cat's hair. She is bending down and brushing the front of his trousers with the palm of her hand when David comes back into the prompt corner ready to fly the tabs. He has another pang of jealousy when he sees Sally being so close to Edward.

Neither of them seem to be in the slightest embarrassed by being caught in this almost intimate situation. David finds that their continuing casualness aggavates him still further. He feels that they are all, Sally, Edward, Adrian Birkett, ignoring him and his private fantasy. The envy of their easy and naural relationship has been growing for months, and the last day has exaggerated his awareness of it. Through habit he checks the tabs are correctly in their 'in' dead, though it is only minutes since he flew them in after the floor sweeping, before sinking into a jealous sulk. He leans against the steelwork of the safety curtain track feeling like an outcast and aggravated by the sensation. The cast are stirring in their rooms, awaiting the 'beginners' call.

Glenda is pondering the other cast members and their relationships as is her habit. She has convinced herself that Steven and Julia may be starting what she coyly thinks of as 'a relationship'. She is saddened by this, fearing Steven to be too predatory for the young girl. She comes to the conclusion that she dislikes Steven. He seems to her to be capable of both calculated seduction and vicious annoyance if he doesn't get his own way. Vicious? Yes, she thinks, that is the right word. It's a most unatractive trait. Not at all the right sort of person for Julia to whom she has attributed an innocence which she would find inaccurate if she knew all of the girl's past liasons. Julia's youth, relative to the rest of the cast causes Glenda to think, quite wrongly, of her as a naive child.

She sits wondering who from the company would be a better match for the girl. Not Alan, surely. And Gregory is strangely involved with Jessica. She bristles a bit at the thought of Jessica. There is the unspoken rivalry between them, unneccessary, Glenda thinks, as in her mind the only claim to status Jessica has is having been in the pre London tour. She can't actually remember how or why this competition between them began. She probably noticed it initially at the inevitable press nights and first night parties where, accustomed to being effortlessly the 'grande dame', the de-facto leading lady, she found Jessica pushing forward for handshakes. It was a new experience for her after long years of her seniority being tacitly accepted.

Her thoughts drift to Adrian. Adrian is married, but Glenda knows that he and Anne are not really on speaking terms, in fact she wonders whether they are actually living together at all. There is something dangerous about him she feels. He is too self confident, and despite all the months the show has been running she has failed to gather any firm information about his more distant past. There is plenty of current gossip, and even in her mostly lonely separation she hears names of girls, usually from shows in neighbouring theatres, associated with him briefly. Further back seems deliberately obscure. There is some salacious past there she is sure.

The beginners call breaks through her day-dreaming, and she gets up to make her way to the stage, checking her appearance as she leaves her room with professional thoroughness. It is not her call yet, but tonight she thinks she will watch the opening from the wings. Cusiosity means she wants to see how Julia and Steven are treating each other. She takes up her position at the top of the lead-off treads where she can watch without being particularly observed herself.

Julia meets Steven in the corridor that leads to her dressing room. It doesn't occur to her to ask why he is so far from his own room just as they are about to go up on tonight's performance, she is more intent on telling him what she feels about his sneaking away during the night. The possibility that he was coming to see her doesn't cross her mind.

"Why did you just leave, without even saying goodbye?" she demands.

"I didn't want to wake you, you looked so peaceful."

"All right then, why did you leave at all? Didn't you have a good time?"

They are standing close together now, so she has to look up at him. It seems to place her in an inferior role. It redoubles her annoyance.

"You know we did."

"Well what was so damn important that you had to sneak away?"

"I didn't 'sneak away', I told you, I didn't want to wake you, and I had things to do."

"What things?"

Steven isn't about to explain himself at the moment. He has some guilt about what he has been doing and doesn't feel inclined to share it with this girl. He looks down at her upturned face. Pretty, yes, but suddenly becoming demanding he sees. There are plenty of girls. She is not particularly special to him, though last night was enjoyable. If he could see a way of dealing with his situation without upsetting her he would. Maybe a complete sharp break would be best. After all neither of them thought of last night as the start of a serious long-term affair.

"Actually things that are none of your business. Private things"

"Oh thank you very much!" she hisses at him.

"A bit of sex doesn't give you carte blanche to know everything I do. If you fancy yourself as a some sort of Mata Hari you'll need to try a whole lot harder than that."

"You stuck up bastard!"

"Hey, hey, don't be like that, it's just I had to go and see someone, and I don't want everybody knowing."

"Who?" she asks reluctantly giving in to growing curiousity.

"Honestly you don't need to know. Maybe nothing will come of it, so I don't want to discuss it, well not yet anyway."

"You can't just fob me off like that."

"All right. There isn't time now, but I'll come and find you in the interval." He thinks that she is going to become demanding. Better to get things under control.

Julia is not much mollified by this, but the show is about to begin. Still smarting from what she feels was a snub she readies herself for another performance.

Sally has her lighting and sound operators on the end of her 'cans'. Douglas has given her front of house clearance. She replaces the receiver of the phone. Near the centre doors to the circle the house manager does the same.

"Houselights Go."

David, holding the tabs rope takes the brake off.

The audience quietens, rather reluctantly she thinks, as the houselights go out.

"Sound Go." and as she can hear the music fade she makes her habitual 'up' gesture to the tab-man who pulls upward on the hemp rope and the tabs fly out. As the curtain goes up she says:

"LX cue 1 Go"
to the operator as David is pulling, and, as the curtains rise the eletrician lifts the front of house inhibitor so light from the audience side of them is added to the preset to establish the scene.

She judges the moment for the doorbell, and the show is under way once more.

Sally fills in 'time up' on the sheet.

Chapter 9

David secures the tabs with the brake and looks at Sally, but she is writing on the show log and fails to acknowledge him as he leaves. His feelings about her contact with Adrian yesterday continue to grow due to what he sees as her ignoring him. He will sit in his room as the show proceeds nursing the seeming injustice of the world.

Maid: Oh, Mr and Mrs Burke. Please come in. Mrs Morgan-Burke will be down very soon. Have a seat in the drawing room. Can I get you some tea?

Julia seems completely normal, thinks Glenda. She can't see the girl's face from this side of the stage. Maybe if she could she might detect a quizzical expression. Julia is still trying to work out Steven's's attitude following his disappearance from her flat last night and their conversation backstage a few moments ago. She is determined to force proper answers out of him in the interval.

Paul Burke: No thank you, Molly. I'll pour us some drinks.

"Miss Johnstone and Mr Hattersley, this is your call."

The too familiar lines flow past.

> *The doorbell rings. The maid enters stage right. She crosses to the door stage left. She opens it.*

Maid: Oh, Mr and Mrs Fathers. Please come in. Mrs Morgan-Burke will be down any moment. Please join the others in the drawing room. Can I get you some tea?

Rita Fathers: Yes please, Molly. (*she enters with Patrick Fathers trailing behind meekly. Molly leaves.*) Paul, how nice to see you, and Wendy of course. Where's Stuart?

Sally gives Edward a look, as if to say 'Are you sure it's just ordinary tea?' but he is off to pour the boiling water into the pot. She relaxes for the long cueless scene with just the occasional call. She has spotted Glenda lurking on the staircase opposite, well back and out of the stage light or audience sightlines. She will give the call anyway, but it's strangely early for the older woman to be there. Sally is conscious of her own comparative youth in this company. In most shows it wouldn't matter at all, in fact the older casts usually relish having young crew to run around after them, but there is so little actual physical work involved in this simple 'murder-mystery' that there is nothing for them to be grateful for.

Perhaps she is, herself, really becoming old and set in her ways. She has a fleeting fear of spending the rest of her working life with this show, cueing the same few lighting and sound cues and calling the same actors to the stage night after night until they are all too old and grey to perform any more. How could you work, for example, on 'The Mousetrap'? The main word there must be 'trap'! She worries that this show is like some theatrical 'Flying Dutchman' condemning them all to an eternity of captivity. She thinks about what she can remember of the opera's plot. Doesn't the ship only come to port every seven years? Can't it only be saved by a faithful wife? A faithful spouse seems so ulikely among this company that she despairs, surrendering to the miserable fantasy she has invented. Glenda's early arrival has unsettled her and she guesses this is just because it is a minor but significant departure from the established routine. She shivvers. The phrase 'someone walked over my grave' pops into her mind.

Does she see relief on Alan's face when he sips the tea? She isn't sure, but there is no doubt that Beth gives the cup a sour look.

Eventually she is able to activate the mic and say, "Miss Wynne, Miss Littlewood, Miss Campbell and Mr Bradford, your calls please."

Soon Jessica and Gregory are in the wing near the props table on her side of the stage, waiting for their entrance through the 'front door'. Sally leans back just enough to see them round the corner of the set and this allows her to see that Gregory is holding the spare gun and Jessica has just grabbed its barrel to steer it away from pointing at her.

'Damn these childish actors,' she thinks, half making to get up and go and remonstrate with Gregory, but he hangs the weapon up again before she can rise.

From her place Glenda has seen the bit of horse-play Gregory was indulging in with the gun. She is not surprised. Boredom is setting in everywhere. She has been more surprised by Jessica's apparent over-reaction as she pushed the gun away, almost as if she thought it was really loaded. It is obvious to Glenda that Gregory completely failed to think about the affect his clowning might have had on the older actress. Now the gun is back on its hook things are more normal on that side of the stage. Does Jessica have a phobia about guns, she wonders. The activity at the moment of the shot each night means that Glenda has never consciously been aware of Jessica's reactions. She promises herself she will make the effort to watch her one night, rather than slipping away from the stage and back to her dressing room while her character is being shot.

Eventually she is on, putting on her character like a coat, 'no,' she thinks, 'like a suit of armour' because she needs protection from the routine:

Eleanor Morgan-Burke: (entering UR) Patrick, Rita... Ah, Paul, and Wendy, of course. How kind of you to come.

Glenda pauses on the staircase, pleased that the rest of the cast turn towards her, though her alteration of the director's positioning of her means they have little choice. She has imposed the change for so long now that the rest of the cast have probably forgotten the original blocking.

Wendy: It's very kind of you to ask us.

Rita: Is that what you were saying earlier?

(*Paul shushes her with his free hand.*)

Paul: You summon us, mother, and we children obey.

Eleanor: You 'children' have never obeyed me...

(*The doorbell rings. The maid hesitates.*)

Paul: Just dump it there, Molly. I'll take it up later.

(*The maid puts the suitcases down and goes to the door to open it*)

Maid: Mr and Mrs Dunsfield, do come in, everyone is in here.

(*Rosemary and Stuart Dunsfield enter.*)

Eleanor: Rosemary. Late as usual.

Rosemary: Sorry mother.

Stuart: That will have been my fault, I'm really sorry Mrs Morgan-Burke ...

Eleanor: Eleanor.

Rosemary: What have we missed then.?

Glenda grits her teeth, because Jessica's make-up is even more strikingly ruddy than usual. She doesn't know that Jessica has been interrupted while making up tonight. She would not consider it an excuse even if she did know. Determined not to betray the irony of the line she concentrates.

Eleanor: Rosemary, you're looking very pale. Are you ill?

Paul: Perhaps she's pregnant.

Rosemary: Paul! You never did know how to behave in polite society.

Eleanor: Well? Are you?

Rosemary: Oh no mother, of course not.

Eleanor: No, I don't suppose you are. None of you seem to be willing to produce heirs for the line.

Rita: Patrick and I aren't married, mother.

Eleanor: That doesn't seem to stop anyone these days. Doubtless you and Patrick will be expecting a double room tonight as usual. Molly, go and fetch Annette to take those bags up, the place looks like a hotel foyer.

(*Molly exits.*)

Paul: Is Annette still here then? I thought you said you would be letting her go.

The scene continues. Eventually Beth and Alan are playing their scene.

Rita: Patrick! That's my mother you are talking about.

Patrick: A mother you say always ignored you in favour of your big brother and little sister.. and she's doing it again now.

Rita: I don't neccessarily wish her dead though.

Patrick: But we need the money.

Rita: Don't remind me. Those people you owe are really nasty. They're going to come collecting one day.

Patrick: I'm likely to wake up with no kneecaps if they do come looking.

Rita: Darling, I will sort it, I promise I will. If she doesn't agree to keep the will as it is we'll just have to find a way to stop her signing the new one. I'll make sure it doesn't get signed.

More of the play, the family's internal bickering is played out to show the various relationships, and the end of the first half approaches. Sally does her calls, puts electrics on standby for the end of the act and tells sound to standby with the interval music. She goes to collect the gun and comes back to her desk. She sees David has arrived by the tab rope while she was away, and nods casually to him by way of a standby. He smiles back, still fantasising.

Eleanor: Rita, sometimes you can be the rudest person I know!

Rita: Well it's true, mother. Why would anyone carry on in a house like this?

Patrick: (*aside to Rita*) Perhaps Annette thinks she is in line for a big share of the will. She might be if she's getting a lump sum. Once the new will is done we're going to be short changed.

Rita: It's going to be Paul who will be quids in.

Eleanor: Annette, can you go and shut the porch door please while my children squabble.

(*Annette goes out through the hall*)

Anne's few moments alone, offstage in the wings and next to the remaining gun have come. She can't break the habit and holds the spare again, turning it over and studying it, feeling its weight and opening and shutting it quietly... considering Adrian, before reluctantly replacing it and going back into the scene with a thoughtful glance over her shoulder at the silent weapon hanging by its cord against the flattage. In the bright lights of the stage scene Glenda is saying;

Eleanor: ... and I'll join you in the dining room in a minute.

(They all exit. Eleanor goes into the study. A pause.)

Strangely Sally somehow fails to see Glenda as she leaves the stage tonight. But the rhythm of the show is engrained in them all. She waits for a count of three from when she thinks the actress has exited, and, with the pistol straight up, pulls the trigger.

The shot rings out in the silence. And seemingly, almost like a second bang from the direction of the dressing rooms, an answering echoing shot seems to sound.

Sally jerks her head toward the nearest door, which is in the wall behind her, confused. But the show runs on as normal, She can see cast members hastening into position ready to cross the stage. The usual pause, the footsteps that must be Julia crossing the stage, and then the scream.

The odd bang has come at that moment of confusion, with cast members moving in different directions in the gloom, that Glenda dislikes so much. Nothing will disrupt the conclusion of the act, it is unstoppable, like a speeding train, yet the whole company has experienced a more than split second hesitation from the unfamiliar noise.

Sally gives "LX cue four, go," and the scene fades to blackout. She indicates to David and, obediently, he pulls. The tabs fly in and she says, "Houselights and preset.." Lights come up on stage, dazzling even after such a short time in blackout. Sally asks sound for the interval music, writes 'time down' for the first half in her record, and turns to Edward and says, "What the hell was that?"

The same question is on everyone's lips, and the overriding consensus after they have all discussed it is that some backstage show relay speaker happened to have been left turned up very high. They all agree that the shot has always echoed along the corridors, and they go to their rooms.

On the way Glenda realises that she has failed to touch the spare gun, shrugs, half laughs at her superstition, and goes into her room. Rosencrantz is standing by the door looking up pathetically at the door knob.

"Hello," she greets the animal, "was that a loud bang tonight? Did it frighten you?" She tickles the cat's chin, feeling the vibration of its purr.

She opens the door and the cat snakes through the widening gap to jump onto her dressing table and begin nosing at her bag.

"Yes, all right. Let's see what we can find for you," she tells it.

She puts a dressing gown on over her costume to protect it and delves in the bag for the daily sandwich. Sometimes she will change out of her costume until just before the curtain call but tonight it seems too much bother. She will just be careful not to spill anything on it, though the wardrobe is always routinely cleaned and maintained. She turns the unruly babble of the interval audence right down and feeds the cat some sliced ham. It is a bit wet from its contact with tomatoes and lettuce in the sandwich, but the cat doesn't seem to mind.

Sally and Edward have come to the same conclusions as the cast, and since, surprisingly, none of the players have come bustling up to the prompt corner, self importantly demanding an explanation, they dismiss it from their minds. Sally doesn't even write a comment in the show log.

The iron hisses in and mutes the sound of chatter, rustling wrappers and ice-cream sales a bit. The cast occupy their interval in their different ways.

The suitcases are moved back across the stage and onto the props tables ready for the next performance. Edward clears tea things from the side table and resets decanters and glasses in their normal positions, adjusts the furniture and plumps up the cushions before vanishing backstage to do the washing up.

Julia has gone to her room and is waiting for Steven. Unsure whether he will make good on his promise to explain things she initially sits at her mirror, but she realises that means her back will be to the door. He will be behind her, and there is the potential in the tiny room for the conversation to be conducted via the mirror. She doesn't want to have to stand up and turn round when he arrives, as if welcoming him. She stands now and fiddles with the hangers on the rail beside her. This way she will be able to shove him back out of the room if his explanation isn't convincing. After all, she thinks, I'm not trying to woo him back. If he wants to go off to his next conquest then let him. A tiny nagging thought at the back of her brain reminds her that last night had been good, and that she had been looking forward to a repeat until she woke up to find she had been deserted.

The noise of the audience on the show relay is a confirmation that whatever dramas are being played out backstage the show is still dragging in reliably large audiences and just for once, actually for the first time in her rather short professional career, she is experiencing the long term security of appearing in a London production with no closing date announced as yet.

She wonders about the people out there in the auditorium that she can hear. There is a babble of voices, muffled somewhat because of the house tabs between the show relay pick-up microphone and the crowd. She doesn't usually give the audience a thought. They are there and in a straight play such as this their reactions do not affect her performance of her minor role. She has even passed the point where she is conscious of them. In the early weeks of this show the behaviour of their audience, composed, as it almost always is for this sort of show, of older patrons did annoy her. The modern tendency to believe that you can talk to your immediate neighbours during a performance had been, and still is, distressingly obvious to her. The hearing deficiencies of these older people also cause comments that were passed to be made in louder voices that are sometimes audible even on stage. Mostly the comments were of the brief, 'I bet he did it,' type caused by a who-done-it. Until she had trained herself to ignore it she hated this. Now she is so oblivious of the public that she wonders if she should start looking for work in film or telly when this run does eventually finish. She thanks whatever lucky star is watching over her that she doesn't need to be thinking about this for months to come.

Steven doesn't knock, he opens the door of her room and comes straight in squeezing her against the chair to close the door behind him. Julia pulls herself back to the present from her introspective musings and tries to assert some control by standing up straight and saying "Well?"

He looks down at her and says, "Now this is completely confidential. No-one, absolutely no-one, must know."

The young actress finds she has been dominated. She nods slowly.

"Promise?"

"Yes, I promise."

"All right. I went to see a casting director."

"Whatever for?" Julia is surprised as this comes so close on the heels of her own thoughts about her security in this show, "I thought 'All Invited' was going to run for the forseeable future".

"Barring accidents it probably is, but I've been offered a lead... big new show opening in the West End soon. It's just about to go into rehearsal."

"But you can't leave this. I mean I assume you're on the same contract as the rest of us, for the duration of the run, aren't you?"

"Yes, and that's where it gets tricky. I wasn't looking for a new part. At least this part of mine isn't exactly much of a role, but I wasn't actively reading the auditions in 'The Stage'. Then I met Emily."

"Emily?"

"She's the secretary for the producers of this new show and we met, and she liked me and put in a word and..."

"You slept with her."

"Yes, but.."

"It's called the casting couch Steven. They have sex with you, promise you'll be hearing from them and then you wait, and nothing happens."

"No. It's not like that. I'm sorry if that's happened to you," he pauses, waiting for her to admit or deny her personal experience of casting. The silence hangs in the air in the tiny room, aleviated only by the background burble of an audience in an interval coming from the relay speaker. She doesn't enlighten him about her experiences, she is wondering how short a gap there had been between 'Emily' and herself. Eventually he continues, "...but Emily passed my number straight to her boss, I went and saw him, and I've been given a part, a lead part, the biggest part. I'm going to be a star."

"But you can't take it. Didn't you tell them that you were in this? Yes you must have done, because they'd have wanted to know about your experience."

Steven nods. He says, "I expect they could re-cast my part pretty easily, I'm not exactly crucial to the play, anyone could take over really. But I imagine that there will be all sorts of threatening noises about breach of contract once I tell them. Best would be if they announced the show was closing. Maybe something will happen to cause it to close early."

"It might be best for you, but not for all the rest of us. What about me? What about any of us. Don't you care?"

She thinks rapidly through her fellow cast members. Her own situation concerns her, but at least she has youth on her side, a very small consolation. It is no secret that they are all fairly mundane actors, there are no real stars among them. Glenda was perhaps, but now well past the age where work would be seeking her out. The Birketts, hardly on speaking terms with each other, Tessa, Beth, Alan, and Gregory trailing around after Jessica like an obedient puppy. No, she thinks, there isn't one of them who could confidently say that they would be able to get work immediately if this show closed.

"Against my own career? Not too much. If someone were to fall ill or die they'd probably close the show." he answers her question with honest self interest.

"You're wishing one of us dead so you can escape your contract! You selfish sod! And you knew about this when you were with me last night."

"It wasn't definite then."

Julia can feel tears starting. She is back to feeling used, she is becoming fearful for her job. She is determined not to let him see her cry.

"Get out!" she tells him, and turns away to hide her face. In the mirror she sees the door shutting behind him. She blinks back the tears. She doesn't want to appear in act two with smudged make up. Her sense of security that this part has engendered has been swept away in one brief conversation. She cannot imagine what Steven could do to arrange the closure of the show for his own convenience, but she worries. Memories of long periods of unemployment and menial jobs to make ends meet come back to her. She wishes she had been more disciplined about putting money aside from this regular income she is presently enjoying.

She only has a minor part, but by most standards the long running London show is paying her well. It is bleeding her finances too, having to have a flat in the capital city, but for the past months she has been comfortable. If by some lucky chance the show carries on she promises herself she will become a saver, but she knows she won't. It never has been in her nature.

Not planning for the future or looking ahead much was the cause of last night's casual fling with Steven maybe. She hadn't thought about any outcomes. She'd seen it as a one night stand, even if his departure had been a mystery that she saw as a slight. Certainly she hadn't expected him to deliver this shock news. She hadn't expected a threat to her security if the show were to close. She hadn't expected to be told he had been sleeping around so close to their night together either. She is not sorry now that he left before she was awake. The quicker and more decisive the break between them the better.

She acknowledges that there has been vested interest in a few of her previous brief liasons. Not exactly casting couch like Steven has been describing, but always, especially when unemployed and seeking work, the background awarenesss that it might be an advantage to be nice to people. And if being nice... No. Well not often she assures herself. Here she is, on 'All Invited to a Murder', in a secure long term job, and she hasn't needed to be nicer to anyone than her nature normally makes her for the best part of a year. In a few curt words Steven has threatened her security and made her feel dirty.

She wonders if she should be warning the other cast members, or at least telling them that Steven is job hunting. Would it be a breach of confidence? He'd said 'confidential' but then aren't they all entitled to know about something with the potential to upset a steady applecart? It can't be kept as his secret if people's jobs are at stake. There is little doubt in her mind that Steven is right, the producers would replace him with a temorary understudy to deal with existing advance sales, and close down as soon as they could. She is still considering this when Sally eventually gives the act two beginners' call.

Chapter 10

While Julia and Steven have been talking the show's daily routine has been continuing. On stage Sally walks to the hallway clock to open its face and wind the hands around to show the audience that time has passed and then does her usual interval check that all is ready.

Back on the prompt side she collects the spare gun and puts it in the case. It feels slightly different tonight. It seems less cold than usual, and she thinks the regular smell of cordite is hanging around more than normal. She opens the gun she has just fired, ah, yes, there's the cordite smell, of course. She throws the used cartridge into the bin below her desk where it makes a metal on metal 'ting' as it goes in, before putting both guns in their box and visiting the stage management room to lock them away. When she returns David is pressing the 'up' button and the 'Act two beginners please' announcement is given to the low background noise of the electric winch motor as the iron rises again, its legal obligation for this perfomance fulfilled.

No Adrian tonight. She wonders if she was anticipating him arriving. She waits for him to come and offer some lame suggestive line. 'No time for a quickie tonight' or something similarly smutty. Still he has proven to be quite good at shoulder massages, even if he does probably have ulterior motives. She knows all about his rumoured liasons. He is excitingly predatory. She wonders if she really minds. His blatant flirting may mean nothing to him, and it may be purely an escape valve for his notorious randiness, but she is half prepared to accept it as flattery. She is not exactly fighting suitors off these days. The working routine that she has severely curtails socialising with anyone outside the profession.

She waits, and he doesn't arrive. Other cast members are in position. The interval has run to within seconds of its allotted time. Lighting, sound and tabs are on standby. No Adrian.

Sally is annoyed. Her repeat backstage call to the dressing rooms betrays urgency by using the formula "Mr Birkett, on stage now please," usually reserved for a crisis. They wait. Still thinking about his shoulder massages and inuendo she feels almost as if she has been stood up. She is annoyed that the string of repetitive time entries on her show report sheets has been broken, but pleased that she didn't enter the times in advance as it had crossed her mind to do. The cast shuffles impatiently. Sally says to Edward, "Go and chase him up, surely even he can manage to find the stage from his dressing room after this length of run."

Edward goes in search of the missing actor. He is secretly pleased that Sally has implied that she doesn't find Adrian very bright, even if it has been said under the stressed conditions of his not responding to a call. Maybe this small blot on his copybook will remove Adrian from Sally's circle of suitors. Maybe... He knocks at Adrian's door. There is no reply. Conscious of the way the interval will now be seeming to drag and the resulting urgency he opens the door and looks round it into the room.

Adrian is lying on his back on the floor.

There is a neat bloodied hole in his forehead.

Edward has never seen a body before, but he needs no experience to realise that the man is dead. He slams the door shut and rushes back to the prompt corner.

Sally spins in the swivel chair at the crashing sound of Edward coming into the wings from the backstage corridor, thinking it will be Adrian and preparing a stern frown for his tardiness, there will be no time for a telling off, she thinks, they are now late going up on the second half. It is very unprofessional of him, but a note in the show log and words after the performance will have to do. She is actually breathing in, ready to tell electrics to take the houselights down. The look on Edward's breathless face freezes her, and he gasps out, "He's dead!"

Chapter 11

It has been a long evening. Sally has had to rouse the front of house manager from the throes of cashing up the interval bars' takes to make an announcement to the audience, a task that could possibly have fallen to Adrian as the show's star name were he not lying dead in his dressing room. Oddly, perhaps, Sally did not consider Glenda to make a front of curtain speech, feeling the situation demanded a more male gravitas. Douglas has carefully managed to inform the audience that the show would not be continuing without saying exactly why, and the partly grumbling, partly bewildered departing crowd are outside in the street now, speculating about the small sea of flashing blue lights in the road beside the theatre. The presence of an ambulance among the police cars in the gathering of emergency vehicles fuels the rumour mill which is running at a high level alongside the bitter discussion about refunds.

Inevitably Sally's priorities have revolved around the show, the audience, and her cast. Informing the authorities, particularly the police, as it was abundantly clear that Adrian was beyond the help of any ambulance, came low on her personal list of jobs to do in this strange situation. In fact she has even made a hurried call to the show's producing management, on their unlisted night-time emergency number, before turning to dialing 999. The police inspector who has taken control of the case takes a very dim view of that and tells her so quite forcefully.

By the time the disappointed audience has left the area, and even the coach parties have been collected by their buses, the stage and dressing rooms have been effectively sealed off by the investigation. The safety curtain has been dropped. Sally has arranged for the pass door to the front of house to be locked, allowing the house staff to be sent home.

Douglas has agreed to a very cursory 'pick-up' by his staff in the auditorium really just to cover any fire risk, and the front of house personnel have been given an early night. Some are debating whether they will get paid a full shift as they leave. Most are unsure when they are expected to turn up for work again. The audience may not have been told why the show has stopped, but word has got out among the staff and spreads within the theatre. Once the house staff start to leave the news will reach the wider world.

Cast and crew are not so lucky and they have found that they are all being kept corralled within the theatre. Reg has been busier than he can ever remember, as the police order him to shut and lock doors and keep him on hand to admit a seemingly endless succession of paper boiler-suit clad investigators. He is torn between irritation at being ordered about and proud importance as he, and he alone, holds and controls keys to different areas. Forensic experts of all types arrive, and eventually leave. The cast and crew are all fingerprinted. The show's guns are seized and taken off for analysis. At some point the pathologist allows Adrian Birkett's body to be removed.

The night grows later, and it becomes evident that they are all under suspicion.

Anne is sitting in Glenda's dressing room being plied with tea. Real tea, brewed by Edward in the prop tea-pot and served in the cups used in Act one each night. He has produced a hip flask of whisky from somewhere and has added a generous dash to Anne's drink. He and Glenda sit either side of her, unsure what to say.

It is Anne who breaks the uncomfortable silence. She takes a sip of the tea, pauses, looks at it surprised, recognises its alcohol content and drinks a generous gulp with the air of one who is afraid it might be taken away from her before she manages to get it all down.

She says, "I can't really pretend to be sorry."

"You don't have to say anything, Anne," Glenda tells her.

"But it is a shock, you know. I've hated him so much for so long now, it's as if I'd had a wish granted."

"I knew you weren't exactly getting on," Glenda admits, slightly shocked at the admission of a death wish and thinking that in Anne's postion she would try to avoid letting the police hear her say anything like that.

"Oh we haven't been together, you know, 'together' since this show opened... not for a long time before that really. He was always out with some girl or other. And there was the book."

"Book?"

"You know, like the song, 'more than a number in my little red book...'," she semi-chants the old hit, "Well he kept all his conquests' names and addresses in a book. It was like him carving notches in the bedpost, rubbing my nose in it, every night..."

Edward stirs uneasily. "Perhaps you girls would rather I went?"

"No, don't be silly," Anne tells him. "It's all going to come out now isn't it? Whoever they decide did it it will be all over the press, and then there'll be a trial, and everyone will get questioned endlessly, in public." She hesitates. "Mummy always told me never to wash my dirty linen in public. I couldn't have arranged a more public situation or dirtier linen really. Jessica's got a line about that at some point hasn't she?"

Glenda and Edward exchange a look over Anne's head as she goes on:

"They're going to say it was me aren't they? I know they are." and for the first time since she was told about her husband's murder her voice rises in pitch and betrays the beginning of hysterical panic, "They're going to hang me aren't they!"

"They don't hang people any more in this country, you know

that," Glenda tells her firmly, trying to calm her.

"Well prison then, oh god! No! I couldn't bear it... I'd rather be hanged."

"No-one's going to be hanged." Edward promises. He feels safe giving that assurance. As for prison, he doesn't know what to tell the actress. Obviously she is going to be a suspect, it seems they all are, and he can see that any detective is going to ask very searching things when Anne and Adrian's marital situation comes out. If Adrian was shot with one of the show's guns then they all had some sort of access to those, and Anne seems to have the most motive by her own admission.

Glenda asks, "Have you got any family you'd like to tell. I think we could probably ask them to contact someone for you."

"No, there's no-one. That's what made things so difficult, I mean I only ever spoke to people in the company, people like you."

The two of them are made to feel guilty that they hadn't made much effort to be friendly to Anne. They exchange looks across her again. Edward finds himself wondering when he did last speak to the woman, and thinking it was probably days ago. Even that was doubtless just a 'hello' in passing. But if she is the murderer, he thinks, the less contact he has had the better. Perhaps it will not be a bad idea to escape from this tête-a-tête before the police notice.

Glenda falls silent too, wondering how her situation will look to the police if their assumptions about when Adrian was shot are proven correct. She had left the stage, and was alone. Her unobserved exit naturally takes a route right past Adrian's dressing room door. She, perhaps more than any of them, has no alibi. An unreasonable chill grips the pit of her stomach, and she regrets Edward not having put whisky in her tea too.

Chapter 12

David Saunders is sitting in his 'office' by the locked pass-door. None of the rest of the resident crew have been detained by the police, because they were demonstrably not in the stage area at the time of the murder. He could seek out Reg and talk to him, but he knows that there is much coming and going by the force and he can do without being looked at, or told to move away, any more than has already happened.

He isn't sorry that Adrian Birkett is dead. For the past day or two he has wished that some magic force would remove the actor, would remove the actor's hands from the shoulders of his fantasy girl-friend, Sally. The image of the man standing behind Sally and massaging her shoulders is burnt into his mind with the clarity that only real jealousy can achieve. He remembers how she seemed to enjoy Adrian's touch, how she closed her eyes and made a small moan of pleasure, while all he could do was stand, uselessly holding the tab rope. He has a guilty, vivid memory of his reactions, of how he felt genuine loathing for the actor, of how he spent that night going over and over the fleeting moment in his mind, trying different things he could have said or done at the time. He could have pulled the actor away, told him to leave Sally alone, put his hands on her shoulders to replace Adrian's, moving firmly and confidently over her back.

But he hadn't. He had stood there like a helpless wimp. Last night at home he had driven himself into a state of frustration that generated a succession of fantasies, some relating to what he wanted to be doing with Sally, some relating to ways he would like to remove Adrian's attentions from her.

Now the man's attentions are gone for good, and he is pleased.

He is under no illusions. Sally remains a distant, unobtainable, wish for him. The actor's death may even signal the closure of the show, in which case Sally will be vanishing from his life as surely as the discarded scenery will be loaded onto a lorry. At least she will not end up with Adrian. He has heard rumours that the man was a serial womaniser. Good riddance.

Jessica is sitting at her dressing table. She has been removing her make-up very slowly and methodically for a long time now, Her eyes are on her image in the mirror but her mind is wandering and throwing up random thoughts about the situation for her consideration. Naturally Gregory is on a chair beside her. They have spoken very little since they retreated to her room to wait. The actress looks damp and saggy in the mirror, a trick of the sheen left by the removal cream she has been smearing around her face and the way her skin is betraying her age having been stretched into loose folds by the fierce wiping she has been doing with the cotton wool and not having yet recovered. Her skin is slow to recover these days.

She drops a last ball of orange stained cotton wool in the bin and puts the red and cream lid back on the tin of remover.

She looks at Gregory's refection in the mirror, then down at the tips of her fingers, where traces of black ink from the fingerprinting that they have all just been subjected to are still visible.

"Your fingerprints are all over that gun," she says finally, with unusual sharpness.

They have discussed it. They have deduced that the spare gun must have been the murder weapon. With its pair it has been taken away and a rush job of ballistics analysis is under way somewhere. Neither of them are sure how much information the forensic examinations are able to extract these days, but both understand fingerprints, and realise that their contact with the weapon will be easily deduced.

Gregory looks unsure, not a normal expression for the younger actor. He usually exhibits an air of confidence. He has been surprised how this has withered since she told him to stop 'fiddling' with her make up.

"So are yours," he answers her, thinking of the sequence of events in the wings earlier.

"Only because I had to push it aside when you were horsing around with it."

He realises he has been foolish to leave his prints on the gun. He wishes he hadn't played about with the weapon.

Gregory watches as Jessica stands and puts her blouse on. She has been sitting at the table in her underwear after taking her costume off. He doesn't offer to leave or turn away while she dresses. He has seen this process so often it is just a background. She doesn't attract him at all, her heavy body, clad in pale pink old-lady bra and pants is uninteresting.

Dressed, she begins doing her hair, brushing the grey strands to get rid of the style that has been forced on her for her part. The nightly process of shaping and restyling has not helped and she knows her hair is thinning. Her hairbrush is regularly full of grey hairs.

"Anyway," he says, trying to appear confident, "neither of us killed him."

"How do you know?"

"Why would we?"

"I might have been having a torrid affair with him..."

"Oh for goodness sake!"

"Or you might."

"I'm not gay.. I don't think poor Adrian was either. There were rumours that implied quite the reverse."

"So he went off with someone you fancied and you were jealous."

"Oh really! You know that's nonsense."

"I only know that if I try I can dream up a plausible reason for almost anyone in the company to be the culprit. If I can so can the police, and our prints all over that gun aren't going to look good. We're very likely to become suspects."

Gregory seems worried by this. Jessica's only real concern at the moment is that she can forsee their enforced captivity here in the theatre being extended for the forseeable future. She would greatly prefer to go home to her flat. She feels too old to be spending the night here. Like all theatre people she has occasionally experienced long drawn out rehearsals and run throughs that have dragged into marathons in the past, but this has come unexpectedly, in the middle of a steady routine run, where habits have formed and her expectations of a time for getting home are entrenched.

"I didn't want to stop up all night here while we all get questioned," she grumbles petulantly. Even as she says it she realises how petty it sounds against the incident that has caused her temporary incarceration.

Beth Johnstone is alone in her room. Like Jessica she is staring at herself in the mirror, mainly because the layout of dressing rooms means that the furniture tends to face that way. She has changed into street clothes. Like all the cast she has been told of the death by a mixture of the rumour mill and a personal visit to her room by Sally. She is touched that Sally took it upon herself to visit everyone in the early minutes after the discovery and the audience announcement, rather than simply giving the cast the news by tannoy. She realises that Sally must have bourne the burden of dealing with the management, the staff and the police. Beth is sorry that the young girl has had to deal with all this, for to her

Sally is a very young girl.

Her expression reflected in the mirror is sombre, serious. Her hands are shaking. Shock is slowly setting in across the whole company as the news sinks in.

Things have quietened down at the stage door. The arrivals and departures have ceased. The night watchman has been turned away and Reg has been instructed to make sure the doors remain locked. A solitary uniformed policeman is guarding the narrow porch which has become festooned with blue and white striped tape. A police car is parked by the pavement, though its flashing blue lights have finally been turned off. The policeman is fending off approaches by a handful of news reporters by remaining completely tight lipped. After a while he is joined by a WPC and the two of them are keeping a silent watch over the street and the loitering and inquisitive press.

Some time later a television crew appears, with cameramen and some lights, and, finding there is no information to be gained from the stage door guard, a reporter proceeds to do a piece to camera based purely on hear-say acquired from the public in the street. When the piece is completed the crew moves around the corner to shoot footage of the front of house, which is, by now, dark and locked.

They don't know it but Douglas is inside in his office, finishing the daily reconciliation figures, and making phone calls to the venue's owners.

They train their lights on the red and white sign, featuring the title 'All Invited To A Murder' with great irony in their report, and using shots of Adrian's picture on the theatre frontage. When edited together with some biographical material about Adrian gleaned from the files the report will occupy two or just possibly three minutes of airtime on breakfast news. Showbiz stories always sell, and a showbiz murder is exceptionally good grist to the insatiable news machine.

The cat is restless around Reg's feet. He has been told not to open any doors, but Rosencrantz needs to go out. Taking a decision Reg goes along a little used passageway that crosses the rear of the building to a plain and neglected panic exit. He pushes gently on the bar, and with a clank the latch releases and the door creaks open a few inches to allow the animal out. Rosencrantz stops, half in and half out of the door, looking from right to left and back.

"Go on, out you go!" Reg encourages it, and Rosencrantz pads silently out into the weed encrusted area behind the theatre.

Reg pulls the panic exit shut behind the cat and gives the push-bar a sharp tug to re-latch it before returning to his post. His absence has not been noticed.

Sally is sitting on the set. Now the immediate activity that followed the discovery of Adrian's body is over and she can stop for a moment she too feels the reaction from the shock. She finds she is trembling, though the stage is still more than comfortably warm despite the working lights having taken the place of hot stage lighting and the audience, normally a reliable source of warmth during a show, having been sent away. She remembers having been told that each member of the audience is equivalent to a sixty watt bulb in giving off heat, so a full house in this theatre.... Sixty times about a thousand is like... How many electric fires? She abandons the mathematics. Mental arithmetic is not at the forefront of her mind at the moment but she knows from experience how quickly a venue will cool once it is deserted at night. This venue is not deserted tonight though.

The stage is a welcome familiar place to sit. The set is more opulent than her one bedroom home, and she has probably spent more time enclosed by its fake walls, doors, windows and staircase than she has in her London flat. There are only three walls really, for the fourth wall would normally be the audience, though now that opening is closed off by the pale ecru lining of the house tabs, puckered at the bottom by the weight of the chain pocket. She leans back in her chair looking upward. Above her a piece of false ceiling hangs masking part of the void that stretches up into the darkness of the fly tower. The ceiling piece is a bit dusty she notices, and the mouldings on it are clinging to traces of greyish dust that don't normally show under stage lights. There is other dust all around now, on doorposts and handles, where the fingerprint people have swirled their soft brushes leaving white powder everywhere. Sally muses over how pointless this is. All their fingerprints must be everywhere. Their long association with the show must mean there can be no part of the backstage, or the scenery or props, that every individual couldn't have legitimately touched at some time. Well perhaps the guns, but one way or another everyone seeems to have had those in their hands at some time.

She remembers seeing the forensic men, in their white paper suits, crawling around on the stage floor and poking into every item on the props table. They had powdered every part of the set for fingerprints and photographed the most obscure parts of the set and backstage. She can't begin to imagine what all this activity could possibly tell the detective, except that for the past forty odd weeks, every night and twice on Saturdays, the same handful of people have worked, performed and moved about in these few square feet of stage space. It must be like examining a family home, for that is what the set represents, and expecting to deduce anything about the movements of the occupants. If they have come up with fingerprints that do not match the company they have not said so.

The scene is standing ready for an act two that will not now be played. She and Edward had re-set before the shock discovery. Upstage the windows show her a painted cloth which serves as a representation of the garden outside the house. By theatre standards it is a small cloth, needing only to be big enough to fill the area that can be seen from the auditorium through the perspex glazed french doors. She thinks of how realistic it looks during LX cue two when the changing lighting state is on it, and how that illusion is completely destroyed now, so it looks like exactly what it is; a drab piece of painted canvas.

She compares it mentally with the view from her own window, and is shocked to realise that she finds the outlook from her home hard to visualise while the fake world she inhabits at work is so clear and memorable.

Her shivering intensifies, and she gets up, desperate for something to do to distract her and get the silly reaction under control. As she does so Detective Inspector Carl Fenton comes onto the stage. He is looking around and, because he is an outsider to the stage world he is drawn to look upwards to the vast spaces above and to either side of the set that the public never see.

Chapter 13

She says, "Hello inspector," and believes for a moment that she has made him jump.

"Ah, Miss Jenkins."

He is wearing a lounge suit rather than a uniform, though you would probably guess his profession on sight. He grips the bottom edge of his jacket and pulls it sharply down to smarten himself. She decides she doesn't like him, though she has to admire his ability to remember her name. The circumstances are not in favour of him, but there is something chilling and formal in his attitude. He is a heavy man with short, cropped, hair which has been so thoroughly cut that the bulging flesh at the back of his neck is exaggerated and pronounced. He fixes the girl with a hard stare.

"Since you are here can you talk me though what would have been happening here at the time Mr Birkett was shot?"

"I don't know when he was shot, but I presume you think it was at the same time as the stage shooting."

"I've spoken to a couple of your cast," he consults a small black flip over notebook, "Miss Fanthorpe and Miss Varley... They happened to have been the first I have interviewed. And they both say that there was a second shot at the about the same time as the one in the play."

"The sound was a bit unusual, yes. At the time everyone thought it was an echo from the backstage show relay system..."

"The sound of the show is broadcast backstage?"

"Yes, always. I give the cast their calls over the same system from the desk, there," she points to the prompt desk, "so there are speakers in the corridors and all the dressing rooms."

"And tonight there was the noise of a second shot?"

"Well not really, not a second shot, it was as if the proper gunshot happened again on the speakers a fraction later. It's very difficult to describe. Like an echo."

"How does the sound get to the speakers?"

Sally points up, "There's a microphone up there."

She sees that the stage manager's desk has gone dark, its rows of tiny indicator lamps no longer illuminated. Presumably electrics turned the power off at their end when they were herded out of the building with all the rest of the staff and patrons who had not been backstage. At least the cast will not be trying to eavesdrop her interrogation by this man.

"And is there usually a delay?"

"I don't think so, I mean why would there be? Anyway I don't hear it because I'm here on stage. So I don't really know."

"Explain to me where everyone is when the shot is fired then."

She thinks before replying.

"It's actually a bit confused, Glenda goes off there," she indicates the study doorway, "and then there's the bang, then everyone comes on from entrances over there and Julia screams and we go to black-out and that's the end of the act."

"Everyone?"

"What?"

"You said 'everyone comes on'?"

"Well everyone involved in that scene. Not Mr Birkett, of course, because he doesn't, well he didn't, appear until act two; and Miss Birkett, That's Adrian's wife.. you did know that didn't you? Well she's been off this side just before that so she crosses to OP just before, and then the others come on. But all the rest, they come on from that side and Miss Littlewood goes off this way."

"Let me get this straight. Miss Littlewood's character is killed off-stage, so she has gone before the gunshot, and the rest of the cast don't enter until after the shot."

"That's right."

"So any of them could have done it?"

"They'd have to be very quick."

"But Mr Birkett's dressing room is only just outside there. Where are you and your assistant at this point?"

"I stand about here so I can see Miss Littlewood leave."

Fenton moves to where Sally has indicated and says, "and she goes off there?" A nod. "It's not easy to see."

"No, it's a bit awkward, but it's usually all right, most nights anyway."

"Then you fire the gun?"

"Yes."

"Tonight was perfectly normal was it?"

"Well actually I didn't see Glenda tonight, but it's all so routine that I timed the gunshot from when I would have normally seen her. I knew she'd gone through the study door, so she'd have been hidden from the audience. It would be a bit silly if I'd fired and she was still walking about on stage. I can't imagine Miss

Littlewood being pleased if she had to improvise dying in view! Anyway I point the gun at the roof and fire. Then, as I said, I wait for Molly, Miss Wynne, to come on, go through the door, and scream and then the others come on and I give the cues for the blackout and the curtain."

"Are you watching the stage though all that?"

"Honestly? Probably not. I'm cueing electrics over the headphones and giving a hand-signal to David on the tabs. I suppose if I am honest about it it's all happening on autopilot... like when you make yourself a coffee or something, you probably don't actually remember filling the kettle."

"Where is Edward while this 'autopilot' goes on then?" She gets the impression that in Fenton's world nothing happens on autopilot, that he would recall every move he made, and expects the rest of the population to do so too. An admission of there being any possibility of not having been paying detailed attention seems to prompt suspicion in the detective's mind. Clearly Fenton doesn't work in a field where repetition breeds a less than precise recall of your every move.

"It depends, sometimes he makes a start on the interval scene change. There's lots of things he can do in the wings to get things ready. I think tonight he was near me."

"You only think."

Sally bridles at the implicit criticism. "He was near me as soon as the tabs were in."

"That's all very helpful," says Fenton, though his supicious tone doesn't reflect what he is telling her. "What do you know about this bloke David Saunders?"

"David? Oh he belongs to the theatre, rather than the show. He's here to deal with the house curtains and keep an eye on the place.

Very quiet. I think he's a bit shy. He doesn't talk to us much. He's quite cute really."

"Did he ever talk to Mr Birkett?"

"Not that I know of, I doubt he knew him at all except as a face in the crowd, so to speak."

"Well that will do for the moment. I've got to talk to the others."

She stops him as he is turning away. "It's getting late, is there any way we could send out for some food for the cast?"

Fenton scowls, and then relents and says, "Have it delivered to the stage door, I'll tell my people to take it in for you."

Using the same outside line phone at the prompt desk that she called the emergency services on she dials a fast food delivery number from a yellowed, dog-eared, card above the desk. Placing an order she pulls out her purse for a credit card to pay. She dithers, eventually deciding to use the show's company card rather than her own private one. She knows that the basic rule for a petty cash item would be for her to pay, and then reclaim later through the slow and cumbersome office system. 'Sod them,' she thinks, 'we can argue it out later.' but she feels it would be unfair of the producing management to begrudge the cast and crew some food under these circumstances.

Chapter 14

Fenton works his way slowly and carefully through interviewing the cast and crew. He allows the unusual informality of some of them being engaged in eating slices of the vast quantity of assorted pizzas Sally has ordered in for them while they are being questioned. He is conscious that he too has had his own evening, and his dining, disrupted and is envious of the suspects. He has not been offered any of the food. By the time he has spoken to a few of them he doesn't feel he would want it anyway. The wedges of pizza that are not yet eaten have cooled and dried in the big flat square boxes, with cheese hardening on the top of them till they look as if they have assumed the consistency of the very boxes they were delivered in.

He thinks of the cast and crew all as suspects, though it would probably have been impossible for some of them to have committed the crime. He has talked to Sally again and made her show him how you could get from one side of the stage to the other behind the backcloth without going into the dressing room corridors, though she has been most insistant that it would be impractical. He's not wholly convinced.

He hears the same tale from all of them. A normal performance with a minor glitch with what sounded like a second shot, and then surprise when the victim failed to appear after the interval for the start of the second act.

His instincts tell him that Adrian Birkett was disliked by more people than just his wife. The interview with her has been very uninformative. To start with Glenda Littlewood has insisted on staying with Anne Birkett while he speaks to her. Perhaps with hindsight he is pleased that she did. Anne Birkett was on the verge of hysteria by the time he spoke to her. He thinks at first that this is due to the death of her husband but the conversation shows she has few regrets about being widowed.

He has started with the well worn platitudes, 'very sorry for your loss', 'I know you must be upset, but I need to ask a few questions'.

Before long she is telling him that she was not sorry he had died.

"We were leading very separate lives you see. He was out overnight more often than not anyway, with some woman or another. He kept a book of them, did you know. Names and numbers dating back years. If he couldn't get a date from some chorus girl in a show locally he'd ring up old flames. You wouldn't believe it but they'd still come running years after he'd dumped them."

"Was he out last night?" he asks.

"Yes."

"Do you know who with?"

"I thought it might be Julia, you know, she plays the maid, but that was only a guess. Probably just someone he called up from another show. I never did know for sure who he was with."

The woman gives a suppressed sob. He sees that this is not from grief at her husband's death but comes from a long drawn out period of feeling neglected and two-timed by him. He wonders whether everyone knew about Adrian's womanising. The word 'philandering' pops into his head. It is a bit old fashioned and he is distracted by turning it over in his mind.

Anne is saying to Glenda, "You knew didn't you, tell him what Adrian was like."

Fenton stands, feeling that he will get little more from this interview. His bulk looms over the woman. It seems very threatening to Anne and she blurts out, "Tell him I didn't do it!"

Glenda makes some gentle soothing noises, but the new widow is too distraught and fearful to be comforted.

Glenda says to Fenton, "I don't think she could have done it. She'd have had to pass me with the gun, as I was going off, to get to his room and back, and I didn't see her."

"Are you saying you didn't see her at all?"

"Oh she was there, she has to go off, you see, because my character sends her to shut the porch door right at the end of the act."

Fenton is struggling with these fragmentary explanations about who went where, when and with whom, and though he accepts that the rehearsed and repetitive nature of this long running show means that everyone's movements are predicable and can be mapped he is bamboozled by the thespians' casual use of stage terminology which he finds himself slightly annoyed at.

He is also starting to be aware that despite its apparent solidity this scenic representation of a house offers a number of access points where in a real building there would be brick walls. He has been lulled into thinking that some places would be inaccessible to the murderer simply because the set designer has made it look that way. He thinks back to Sally Jenkins' flat statement that it would be impractical for anyone to go behind the backcloth. He still doesn't understand why.

Deciding there is little more to be learned from the two actresses at the moment he leaves them.

As he walks away he can hear Anne shouting, "I didn't do it! He's got to believe me, I didn't do it!"

In the maze of passages rear of house he comes across two more of the cast, sitting side by side on one of the staircases with a nearly finished pizza in its box between them. Steven offers Fenton a slice of pepperoni, which he declines even if his hunger is growing. The take-away delivery has resulted in the backstage taking on a faint odour of food, and it is constantly reminding him that he hasn't eaten. He will wait it out. He needs to be here for when the initial forensic and pathology reports are brought to him, and it is convenient to keep the suspects all confined to this very precise enclosed area for as long as he can.

Fenton establishes who they are and discovers that they are rather dismissive of the event which has just interrupted the show. One of them makes a half joke saying "'Death imitates art' to misquote Oscar Wilde." Maybe it's a kind of protective reaction to shock at the murder. Maybe they just don't care about the victim. He doesn't know yet.

"You were both on stage when you heard the shot?" he questions them, wanting to return to a question and answer situation.

They start to speak together, but pause, and wait for each other. Steven gestures 'go ahead' to Alan by waving half a segment of pepperoni at him.

"Not on stage exactly, but somewhere in that vicinity," Alan says.

"Same here," says Steven with his mouth full.

"When you say 'in the vicinity' what exactly do you mean?"

Steven swallows and tells him, "Someone will have told you that plays, shows, are exactly the same every night." Fenton nods. "Essentially that's true. In rehearsal every move we make is gone over again and again till it becomes cast in stone. Same with the script, of course. So we can all tell you exactly where we are on stage for any given instant in our current show. But unless it involves a quick change or some scenery moving, which doesn't happen in this play, or someone needing access what we do once we are off isn't laid down. I expect that if you ask her Sally can come up with the notes on the blocking, that's where people move to, from the original rehearsals.. it all gets written down. But this sort of show there won't be any mention of who goes which way once they exit. Right Alan?"

"Absolutely. There's no point."

"Ask anyone in the company and they'll all tell you that it's a bit of a muddle at the moment when Glenda gets shot. For a start we've all gone off in different directions, supposedly for dinner, or to get ready for it.."

Fenton feels another moment of hunger at the mention of dinner. He leans on the handrail, a plain steel scaffolding pole painted white and bracketed to the brickwork. Being a step or two below where the actors are sitting has reduced his usual stature advantage. Although he is still a heavyweight presence he is not dominating the conversation. He knows how he normally appears, and wonders if this relative shrinking is why these two are being so forthcoming with him. His suspicious mind also considers the posibility that guilt is making them try to create a smokescreen of detail around the killing. They may not be the innocent bystanders that they seem.

"...Some of us go out of the OP door, some up the stairs, but that means we've got to come down again by the lead-offs, Glenda goes into the study by that door upstage prompt.. oh and Anne has just been sent out of the porch."

"And we all have to come back on again from different places almost at once," Alan puts in.

"For a few moments each night it's like a tube station in the rush hour back there," Steven tells him, and he waves his hands back and forth to show what he means. The pizza box and remaining slice wobble on the edge of the step and he just grabs it before it sheds its contents down the stairway.

"I don't think it's ever exactly the same twice. It's a bit of a mess really."

"But you'd all know who passed you?" Fenton wants to check.

"Maybe. Think about it like the underground. But it's quite dark, and it's crowded. Would you know who you passed on a platform as you were running for a train?"

Fenton sighs. He pulls his weight off the handrail and stands up to his full height. Pulling the bottom of his jacket down to tidy himself as is his habit he tells them, "I'll be needing you all together soon, I suggest we meet on stage in about half an hour." He looks at his watch, nods to the two of them and makes off.

Chapter 15

Detective Inspector Fenton has comandeered the desk on the set. He has been joined by a uniformed officer, who stands stolidly with his hands behind his back, unemotionally watching. Fenton is clutching an untidy pile of papers that he has been looking at. Unconsciously he is mirroring the exact set-up that forms the basis for act two of 'All Invited To A Murder'. It is precisely here that Adrian Birkett spent the bulk of his appearance as Detective Inspector Palmer in the play. Like Adrian used to do, Carl Fenton perches on the edge of the desk. It creaks under Fenton's weight but he still sits on it, watching the suspects come in, in pairs and on their own, and find themselves somewhere to sit. The addition of the crew means that there are not enough chairs to go round, so Edward goes and fetches a small pile of stacking chairs from the adjacent dressing rooms.

"Did you want Reg as well?" he asks Fenton when he has spread these out.

"Of course. Everyone who could have been here at the time." Fenton is snappy. Edward wonders if he is nervous about the coming interview with all of them together. He heads toward the stage door where Reg is in his accustomed place. He avoids looking at Adrian's dressing room door as he passes it, it is draped in blue and white police tape despite the forensic team having left. Edward thinks that maybe Reg, safe in his stage door office, is the only person here who seems relaxed about the whole situation. He alone seems not to expect to be interrogated, it is almost cruel to spoil his evening.

Edward looks at his watch, and sees that it is not really 'evening' any longer. Now they are in the small hours of the morning and the night is half gone.

He goes out of the prompt side door and down the short flight to stage door level. The door between these stairs and the lobby near Reg's small office bears the words 'Fire Door Keep Shut'. It is wedged open by a square steel stage weight tonight.

"Reg," he says as he walks toward the tiny office.

Reg looks up, smiles, lays the paper aside and says, "What can I do for you Edward?"

"Sorry Reg. That copper is holding some sort of meeting on stage, and he wants everyone to be there. Including you it seems. Do you mind coming?"

"Do I have a choice?" Reg asks.

"Probably not. I suppose they're only doing a job, but this bloke Fenton is pretty hard, he conceals it behind a gentle enquiry sort of thing, but I wouldn't want to cross him."

Through force of habit Edward slides the stage weight away from the door as they make their way to the stairs. The auto-closer swings the maroon painted door shut behind them now it is freed. There is an unpleasant impression of being incarcerated.

They go onto the stage together. It is quite an experience for Reg, for through all the years he has guarded the door he can count the number of times he has stepped right onto the stage itself on the fingers of one hand. He is struck by the ring of serious faces sitting on assorted chairs around the stage, facing Fenton at the desk. From where Reg and Edward have come onto the stage, through the doorway to the porch they have the back of the house tabs ahead of them and the main part of the set, with the desk-perching detective, to their right. Edward points and guides Reg to a vacant stacking chair.

Some of the cast nod to him, and he thinks someone mutters 'Hello Reg'. He feels uncomfortable sitting with the asssembled cast. He is only accustomed to them as fleeting passers-by in his domain at the stage door. Now they sit around like participants at a séance, not talking to each other, and almost obviously avoiding eye contact with their neighbours. He finds himself similarly silent and not looking at the others. Fenton has managed to make them all even more uneasy than Adrian's death has already done. He is glad that his seat is near David's. There is a feeling of the pair of them belonging to the theatre itself and being somehow aside from the company that has suffered this situation. Ever since the activity near the stage door died down he has been mentally playing detective, hoping to guess the culprit. Reg is confident in his own innocence, but once he has given it some consideration he has decided that he alone, possibly, has no real alibi and the easiest access to Adrian's dressing room of any of them. He doesn't believe David would have had anything to do with it, though he thinks that the tabman is sweet on Sally. But Adrian never arrived or departed with her, and Reg is unaware of any connection between them. It seems an unlikely link.

The air in the theatre is now becoming cold as the heating has turned off automatically. Reg thinks wistfully of the old electric fire under the shelf in the doorkeeper's hutch. It is virtually antique, a heavy green enamelled casing enclosing spiralling heater elements supported by and sagging between some ceramic blocks. The elements are so old that they struggle to glow red, but it gives off some heat. Reg doesn't use it often, though he knows the night watchman does. The stage doesn't have any heating of that sort, relying entirely on the building's central heating pipework. He buttons the front of his old tweed jacket, a thing he never does. One of the buttons is dangling from an over-long loose thread. He hopes it won't fall off through being used.

They are all there now, quiet, and waiting to see what the inspector wants to say.

Julia looks very nervous. Her youth is exaggerated by childishly curling up in one of the set's armchairs and wrapping her arms around her knees protectively. She has brought Andy Panda with her and is clutching the soft toy as a comfort. Fenton thinks she might suck her thumb in a moment.

Beside her Glenda is sitting straight backed, managing an air, almost, of disdain at the whole proceedings, but she watches everything and everyone with interest. She is dressed in her street clothes, but has wrapped a dressing gown around her. Looking at her fellow cast members she is struck by how grey and ill the men look. For a while she thinks it is a trick of the unforgiving working lights, then she realises that it is now very late and they are all unshaven. It makes them look disreputable. She wonders if the inspector will be influenced. Certainly if she did not know them she would be reluctant to trust any one of them. She sees though that the same shadowing effect can be spotted on Fenton's face.

Anne is as far from everyone as possible, nursing the solitude she has now managed to achieve by rebutting nearly everyone's sympathetic comments, even Glenda's. Fenton thinks she is trembling, but cannot decide if this is from emotion or cold.

Beth is biting her nails and, like all the rest of them, avoiding any real contact. Edward is sure that the cast have, like him, all decided to try to stay aloof in case they find they have accidentally struck up a conversation with the murderer and become implicated. Like all the rest he is turning the events over and over in his mind, trying to decide who might have wanted Adrian dead, and why. The more he puzzles the more he sees that almost everyone had some reason to dislike the dead actor. Enough to shoot him though? Edward too sits quietly.

Beth shifts about and stretches her arm, wincing at a slight pain.

"Something wrong with your wrist Beth?" Edward asks. His voice seems too loud in the silence.

"Nothing really, I think I've strained it a bit," she says.

Edward pulls out a copy of 'The Stage'. The weekly newspaper comes out on Thursdays, and this is yesterday's edition. Carefully he turns the tabloid to the situations vacant columns.

"Good god, Edward," Sally whispers across to him, "you aren't job hunting are you?"

"I don't reckon this show stands much chance of the run continuing, do you?" he whispers back.

She realises the logic of this and then mutters to him, "Let me know if you see anything for me too."

Edward's depression at having to think about job hunting in the near future is slightly lifted by Sally's words. If he tries he can delude himself into believing that she would welcome them both working on the same show again.

To his right Tessa and Steven are sharing the settee. They have contrived to be at opposite ends of the seat, as distanced from each other as they can. Julia watches him resentfully from her curled position. The shocking event has not replaced Steven's behaviour and their interval conversation in her mind. In fact she feels that Adrian's death, and the obvious threat to the show's continuance that it implies, has somehow been brought about by Steven wishing for a way to escape his contract. The possibility that Steven might have shot Adrian begins to occupy her thoughts. It would be a very dramatic way for Steven to put a halt to the run of the play but he might be callous and selfish enough she now thinks.

Alan has taken a position sitting on the floor by the settee, leaning against the end nearest to Tessa. Like Julia he has his knees up in front of him and is hugging them close to his chest. Fenton thinks that this foetal pose is possibly more protective than due to the chill air.

Fenton eyes them all with equal suspicion. He watches like a cat guarding a trapped bird, ready to pounce on any indication of movement to escape. In his case he is having to watch them all, because he is not sure of his target yet. He is confident that dilemma will be solved for him in the next few minutes. A limited number of suspects, all penned together by circumstances will soon divulge details to him that he needs. Unless, he thinks, they are all in it together. It seems unlikely even if they do nearly all seem to have had some antipathy toward the victim.

The lack of conversation makes it unnecessary for him to call them to order, but he does so anyway.

"Right ladies and gentlemen, I want go through the events of this evening, well yesterday evening now, with you so we can establish the culprit and then we can let you all go home. One of you killed Adrian Birkett. It was a cold, deliberate killing, and rather carefully planned, so the killer had decided on how, and when to do it some time ago. Not an impulse, not a crime passionelle therefore.

"Unfortunately the show you are all appearing in, or working on," he adds, looking about to include Sally, Edward and David and the door-keeper in the accusations, "seems to have provided the means very adequately. Our ballistics lab has rushed through the results and there is no doubt that one of the guns owned by the show was used to fire the fatal shot."

Alan interrupts to say, "That's obvious surely."

Fenton frowns at him. "Nothing about this could be said to be 'obvious'. However there are more aspects to it than just the weapon..."

"There's two guns," Tessa says, "which one was it?"

Fenton hasn't expected to be questioned himself. He wonders what has caused this woman to ask. He shuffles his paperwork and turns back and forth between several sheets of typewritten reports before saying, "The one with the red cord tied to it."

"The spare," Sally says, "It would have to be wouldn't it, because I was holding the other one to fire it for the show."

"That's perfectly true if we believe that the murder happened at the same time as the stage shot," he shifts his weight on the desk, which creaks again.

"And don't you?" Steven asks.

"You have all told me that there was something strange about the sound of the shot at tonight's performance. People have described it as sounding like an echo. Everyone seems to have concluded that the murder took place at that moment. Somehow the murderer timed his, or her, shot to co-incide with the one on stage."

"I should think anyone in the company could have timed it well enough. After all we hear the show night after night and the shot is fairly striking, so we all know when it's going to happen," Sally tells him.

"That assumes that the play is exactly the same every night," Fenton says.

"Well it is."

"Your timings are that closely the same?" he queries, still disbelieving.

"The running time of a whole act is never out by much. If you look at the show logs you'll see that act one runs an hour and four minutes. It's never been an hour and five, or an hour and three. You can set your watch by a show."

"If you say so." It is a phrase that emphasises his doubt. He scans the assembly. They all nod in agreement with Sally's statement. Fenton shrugs. He had not been aware of this regularity of timings in the theatre world. It frustrates him a bit, because he had been thinking that it might have been possible that Adrian had been killed either before, or possibly after, the gunshot was heard, which would have opened up the suspect field yet wider. He remains unconvinced, but in the face of such concerted agreement about show times he decides to go along with the cast.

Chapter 16

"Why did you ask which gun it was?" Fenton asks Tessa.

"I just wondered."

"It couldn't have been the one I use because I was holding it, actually firing it, at the time" Sally reiterates.

Fenton asks her, "Do you find the gun heavy to handle?"

"Heavy?"

"Does it take an effort for you to lift it? Could you hold it straight out in front of you, instead of, as you say, pointing straight up. Is the trigger stiff, or do you have to be careful that it doesn't go off too soon when you are waiting for the right moment to fire it each night?"

"Why?"

"Just answer the question Miss Jenkins."

"Well I could hold it straight out I suppose, but I was always told that, even firing blanks, it was better to point the thing into the air."

"And how sensitive is the trigger?"

"I've never thought I'd accidentally fire it. I mean you do have to mean to pull the trigger for it to go off."

"And both guns are identical?"

"I think so. We only have the second one in case of a misfire, but that hasn't happened. I think it did once or twice on the pre-London tour and the director got nervous about it, so we carry a means of covering a failure."

"Which raises the question, when did you last check the spare was loaded?" I assume you don't unload it each night."

Sally thinks before saying, "No, I don't. There's never seemed to be any point. There's a shell in each gun but only the one I use gets fired, so I assume the spare is OK and ignore it. Though...." She stops again. Fenton waits for her to continue, and then, when she doesn't asks,

"Though what?"

"Well there was a funny thing, Edward and I found a live blamk cartridge on the floor by the bin when we were sweeping up tonight, I mean last night. I don't really know how that got there. If it had been a used one I'd have said that I just missed the bin when throwing it away, but I don't understand a live one."

Fenton leans forward attentively.

"A live blank?"

"Yes."

"What did you do with it?"

"Actually I used it tonight, last night, in the gun that I fire for the sound effect."

"But it made you check the spare?"

"Yes, as it happens, at least, I could see there was a cartridge in it, so I assumed it was OK."

Silently Rosencrantz comes through the doorway from the direction of the study and walks across the stage. About half way he stops, frozen, looking at Fenton. Fenton has seen the cat out of the corner of his eye and stares at it. The detective and the animal try to outstare each other for what seems an age to the assembled cast, until Fenton says, "Where the hell did that thing come from?"

"He belongs to the theatre," says Sally.

"I thought he was still outside," Reg offers, "I only just put him out."

Fenton rounds on Reg, "You put him out? You mean you opened a door?"

"Well just enough for him to go out for a walk. I mean he has to... you know."

"You were told to keep the doors shut." there is a furious rage about Fenton, "And who let it back in?"

There are shrugs all round. Even if one of them has heard the cat and let it in before this interrogation started none of them are now going to admit it in the face of this seemingly aggressive and pointless attack.

Someone mutters, "does it matter?"

Glenda extends a hand to Rosencrantz to encourage him to come to her, but the cat has won its staring competition with Fenton and walks unconcernedly to Reg before jumping onto his lap. Glenda is disappointed. She would have welcomed the distraction. In any case she feels it is fickle of the animal to take bits of her sandwiches every day and then ignore her. From Reg's point of view it is obvious, it is he and the night-watchman who have always fed Rosencrantz, and cats' affections are led by their stomachs. He scoops the animal into a comfortable place on his knees and strokes it as it settles contentedly and closes its eyes.

Sally says to Edward, "See, I told you he doesn't love you any more."

Edward has no time to reply before Fenton says angrily, "Can we please concentrate on the murder! And when I said keep the doors shut, I meant keep them shut."

Feeling resentfully like naughty schoolchildren the company turns back to the matter in hand ignoring a muttered "Yes sir, no sir, three bags full sir" which is barely audible but seems to come from Steven.

The detective jumps off the table and paces up and down before turning abruptly to Gregory. The fury that Rosencrantz's appearance has caused in him is still evident in his tone of voice as he asks,

"Why have you been holding the spare gun?"

Gregory becomes all bluster.

"Who says I have?"

"Never you mind. Answer the question."

Sullenly, reluctantly, Gregory admits to him, "I might have picked it up."

"From which I have to conclude that the guns just lie around unattended, is that right?"

Sally is stung by the implication and says, "Yes he picked it up, and I saw him and told him to put it down. They're not 'unattended'."

"Did you? Why? When was this? What happened?"

"It was during the show, he and Jessica were waiting to go on, and he unhooked the gun and pointed it at her and she pushed it aside."

"What did you say to him?"

"I didn't actually speak, I sort of got up to go over and he saw me and hung it back on its hook."

"Is that right Miss Campbell?"

Jessica is reminded of Gregory's mucking about. She has been trying to forget it, partly because she doesn't want to be reminded of how much it frightened her when she found the gun pointed toward her, its black and venomous looking barrel aimed straight at the middle of her body in the off-stage semi darkness. She is ashamed at the foolishness of her childish flashback reaction to having the weapon aimed her way, for her logical mind had known it was only loaded with a blank, but she can still remember the chill of panic that had taken her over. She hadn't been aware of Sally rising to remonstrate with Gregory because her senses had almost frozen in fear. She can hardly recall reaching out to grab the barrel and push the threat away. She has also tried to forget because the subsequent shooting of Adrian has made her wonder if he died from the same gun, and if so whether it was loaded with a live bullet when Gregory aimed it at her. Their little chat about fingerprints had disguised a deeper worry as far as she was concerned.

Now this hulking hard faced detective is quizzing her about the incident it has brought back the unpleasant ideas she has had since the last performance. Did Gregory know the gun was loaded? If he did was she an intended target? Did he kill Adrian? Did that happen somehow by mistake if the bullet had been meant for her? Or were there more bullets in the gun? These seem to her legitimate questions, especially when she remembers his rather restless demeanour before last night's show. Has she had a lucky escape?

She nods in answer to Fenton's request for confirmation of what Sally has said, wondering if, or how, she should express her doubts and suspicions. But surely Gregory wouldn't kill anyone, why should he? Her thoughts are interrupted by Glenda.

"I can confirm that," the woman announces, "I was the other side of the stage and could see across. Gregory waved the gun about and Jessica pushed it away."

"Thank you Miss Littlewood. May I ask why you were on the other side of the stage? Were you about to come on?"

"Not immediately, but quite soon."

"You were on stage earlier than usual then.. why was that?

"I was watching a bit of the show from the wings."

"And you saw Miss Jenkins getting up to tell Mr Bradford to stop playing with the gun?"

Glenda shakes her head, "No, I couldn't see her from where I was."

Fenton makes a note on one of the sheets of paper he has. The deliberation with which he does this simple job seems to make whatever he is writing very important in the minds of his captive audience. In their individual ways they are intigued to know what he has found worthy of note in the exchange that has just taken place.

"Since, I understand, it is your exit that is the cue for the gunshot Miss Littlewood, I am puzzled as to why tonight, of all the nights, Miss Jenkins says she was unable to see you leave. You arrived on stage early. Miss Jenkins couldn't see you as you exited. Why tonight, and what else was different?"

Glenda has feared this question. She is blustering as she answers Fenton, "I expect I just happened to be a bit quicker getting off than usual." There had been no plausible reason for it, but she has known all along that she had left the stage faster than normal. She also knows that this tiny deviation from the routine looks bad. She is sorry not to have touched the spare gun tonight, it may turn out to be bad luck she decides, illogically.

"I don't like that moment in the play much. There's too much confusion," she tells him, "so I didn't hang about."

"So your change from the established routine may have been why the gunshot timing was wrong?"

"It wasn't wrong," Sally says firmly.

"Oh, but it was," Fenton is definite. "You have all told me that the timings are cast in stone, immovable. If we assume the killer wanted to cover his own gunshot by timing it to coincide exactly with the one in the play he, or she, would have been very careful to make the timing precise. You all tell me that the two shots were a fraction apart, resulting in drawing your attention to them. Had the killer been successful with making the noises overlap no-one would have been aware of a second shot. Miss Littlewood's alteration of her exit, even if only fractionally, made the fatal shot audible. Miss Jenkins' regular routine was thrown and the fractional difference did actually matter in this case. I'm asking myself whether you, Miss Littlewood, could have grabbed the spare gun on the way past and got to Mr Birkett's room in time to shoot him... it is only the next door on the passageway, hardly a marathon sprint, even, you'll forgive me saying, for you."

Glenda adopts her Mrs Morgan-Burke voice in tone and level to say, "I don't see any need for you to be rude Mr Fenton."

Briefly he admires the way her words have cut through the other voices which have started to rise as a background as the others all seem to want to pass comment. He says, "No, I'm sorry, but the fact remains that you could have done it."

The cast and crew murmur uneasily. They are not used to Glenda being attacked. Like her or not she has always been the accepted senior member of the cast, a principal lady despite her fairly brief time on stage. Someone is questioning what advantage there might be in disguising the sound of the shot.

"Because if we didn't know when it happened it makes the business of checking all your alibis much more complicated," Fenton explains, "and you wouldn't miss the victim till he was due on stage."

"Which is exactly when he was missed. So no advantage there," Edward points out.

Fenton shrugs, "The whole of the first act would have been a very wide time period to try to track everyone's movements through wouldn't it?"

"Why would I kill him?" Glenda demands when she can again get a word in.

"Ah. The main mystery here. You all seem to have had the means and to some extent the opportunity but who had a motive?"

"Everyone did, he wasn't exactly popular," Anne says.

Fenton says, "From your point of view wasn't the problem that he was very popular? Wasn't he out with other women every night? Who apart from yourself was upset by that?"

Jessica says, "I couldn't care less who he was dating."

"Yet your prints are all over the gun."

"We've explained that to you."

"But did you know that some of your make-up was on the gun too? I am right that you are alone in using," he hesitates over the unfamiliar trade name as he consults his notes, "Leichner. Is that how you say it?"

"I don't know anything about that," she says.

Gregory clears his throat. "That might have been down to me," he admits. "I left Jessica's dressing room still holding a stick of her greasepaint, then I picked up the gun."

"When, and more importantly why?"

"Before the show started. I just looked at it. Ask Sally," He turns to her pleading, "Tell him Sally."

Sally nods, "Mr Fenton, everyone and their dog seems to want to touch the guns. Yes Greg picked the spare up last night, but I don't know anything about any make-up."

Fenton studies his notes again, "Leichner number 9," he tells them.

"Good grief, I thought she'd have used it all up by now," Beth says rudely. There are a few sniggers.

Glenda mutters "She certainly hadn't run out last night, it was as overdone as always."

"I heard that you old diva." Jessica snipes at her.

The cast begin to join in the dispute, but Fenton asserts his authority, using his sheer bulk to subdue them as if quelling a riot. When they have settled again he says to Sally, "Was it common then for people who had no business with the guns to touch them?"

"They weren't supposed to, but everyone seemed to be really fascinated by them. Sometimes there'd be a few days when no-one touched them, but then they seemed to become desirable toys again."

"Have any of you," he looks all around, "had any experience with firearms?

No-one admits to it if they have. Sally says, "Only on this show."

Jessica says, "They frighten me, ever since I was little. Someone fired at a rabbit in the woods near our house. I was just walking along and there was this bang and bits of dead rabbit on the grass in front of me. Just this man out shooting, but it might have been me! It scared me so much, I didn't even feel sorry for the rabbit, I was just glad it hadn't hit me. I hate guns."

"But you haven't fired one according to what you say?" Fenton is obviously disbelieving.

"Why should I have?"

"You see there is another aspect to this murder. We know that Mr Birkett was shot at very close range. It's one reason we are so sure that it was one of you. He knew you all and would have allowed any of you to be close. The victim was fairly tall, and, you may know by now, was shot in the forehead. To hold one of these guns to someone's forehead you need to be strong enough to stretch you arm out supporting the weight of the weapon," he mimes pointing a gun, stretching his arm out and sticking his index finger out in a playground representation of a pistol, "and to fight against the recoil." he mimes the action of shooting and the gun jerking upward, "In most of your cases you'd be holding the gun above the line of your shoulder to do that. Not easy, unless you were spurred on by a great deal of anger."

"So the killer was one of the men," Tessa guesses, "Gregory? Alan? Steven? Come on which one of you was it?

"I still don't see how any of us could have gone over there," Gregory indicates the direction of the props table, "collected the gun, reloaded it with a real bullet, gone to Adrian's room and shot him and got back in time to be coming on stage for the end of the act."

Fenton feels the interrogation is starting to turn into a discussion. It rather unsettles him. He likes to command. He also likes to stick to one topic at a time. In his experience people discussing something change subjects at rather random moments just like Gregory has done. It always makes him suspect a diversionary tactic. It is a valid question however. Maybe timing rather than physical strength is important here. He decides to challenge the assertion that crossing behind the backcloth would be impossible. He starts by his opinion about loading the gun.

"I think that this murder was planned and prepared for well in advance. I think that the murderer had already changed the ammunition in the spare gun at least yesterday, maybe even earlier. That cuts out any re-loading."

"It might also be where the loose blank that we swept up came from," Sally suggests.

"If that's the case the gun you were waving under my nose was loaded and would have killed me if it had gone off!" Jessica's previous doubts and fears all flood back.

"Very likely," Fenton says, heartlessly.

Jessica gives a little 'Oh!" and can be seen searching for a handkerchief as she starts to cry. Gregory gets up and moves to go and comfort her but she fends him off saying, "No, no, keep away from me!" holding both hands straight out with their palms facing him to keep him as far away as possible. The handkerchief dangles from one hand. Gregory makes some soothing noises, trying again to approach, but Jessica is determined.

Fenton ignores the little scene and says, "I want to see how easy it would be to get across behind that backcloth, because if that is easy then anyone could have done what we have suggested in the available time. Miss Jenkins, you told me it couldn't be done, show me why."

Sally gets up. "I said it couldn't be done without it being obvious, look." and she goes out of the front door, turns around the rear of the cloth and re-emerges though the stage right doorway. It has been the work of only a moment, but the cloth has displayed a clear ripple as the draught of her passing moved across the back of the canvas, wierdly distorting the garden wall image that backs the painted foliage as she passes. "See?" she has been certain in her mind of what would happen, "Even if we on stage didn't notice in the confusion, in the middle of that busy scene, at the time there were a thousand people out there in the audience," she gestures toward the tabs blocking the view of the auditorium, "who would have seen the cloth ripple like that."

"What if you moved more slowly?"

"Doesn't that defeat the object of taking the short cut?"

"Not entirely," Fenton is certain now, "you not only save time, but you're hidden, so no-one spots you. Try it again more slowly."

Sally shrugs, but obediently passes behind the cloth a few more times. Eventually she manages to do this at a speed that causes little or no rippling of the painted material. The change of speed has added less than a second to the journey. Fenton is delighted.

"I think we've established how it was done, then," he declares gleefully, "That just leaves the question of who? You are all experienced performers, you'd all know how the cloth would ripple, so you'd all be able to get behind that cloth like Miss Jenkins just did. Which one of you was it?"

Chapter 17

"You weren't on good terms with your husband then?" Fenton has moved on and is now questioning Anne. It isn't going well for the actress. Her colleagues sit around rather cowed by the man's bombast, pitying her as she is ground down by the incessant queries and surmise. Any objections that were voiced by the others in the early stages of this have been brushed aside and ignored by the detective. Rosencrantz has jumped down from Reg's lap and stalked off the stage in what has appeared to the onlookers as a silent protest.

"It seems to me that you had means, opportunity and motive. You'd prepared the gun at some point the night before, your prints are among those on it. You came off stage, picked up the gun, went to your husband's room, shot him and slipped back across the stage behind the back-cloth, leaving the gun on the table. It was lucky for you that Miss Littlewood varied her usual routine by going to her room more quickly than usual, just plain luck, it made things easier for you, but the plan would have worked even if she hadn't. You told people that you were upset by your husband's address book having names of other women in it. You've admitted that you and Mr Birkett were hardly on speaking terms. You've even said you are pleased he is dead, not the usual reaction to becoming a widow."

"I didn't do it! You have to believe me, I didn't do it!" Anne's voice rises to a panic stricken scream as Fenton starts to recite, "Anne Birkett, I am arresting you...."

There is a hubub. Everyone seems to be talking at once. Fenton's routine speech is drowned out by the cast and crew offering their opinions, joining Anne in her protestations of innocence and giving what are now rather feeble ideas of why she couldn't or wouldn't have done it. Even Reg is on his feet, feeling that if everyone else is standing then perhaps he should too. He wonders how like the show this real late night scene is. Do audiences actually pay to watch this sort of thing?

The uniformed policeman, who has been standing all this time, with his hands behind his back, looking slightly upward at a point somewhere just below the spot bar; passive and seemingly uninvolved, now and seemingly without any instruction, moves towards the woman to reinforce his superior's authority. He hardly needs to, for Fenton's dominatingly brutal appearance is enough of a threat in itself. He is surrounded by the realistic representation of an opulent country house, he continues reciting the well worn phrases of the formal caution above the protestations. The overriding impression is of a bully. Nothing will sway him now.

Beth alone sits still in the midst of all this activity. She is looking down at the carpet that covers the stage floor, apparently absorbed in studying the pattern. She trembles with fear as she says quietly and calmly "I did it."

The confession goes unheard in the rowdiness of multiple voices. The assembled cast have not quietened down to listen to and accept Fenton's words, they have added their objections to Anne's own terrified denial.

Beth raises her voice a bit and says, "I did it!"

The people nearest to her hear her and look at her in stunned disbelief. Slowly the rest become aware that something important has been said, and Beth becomes the centre of attention. The uniformed officer is hesitating, half way to reaching out to handcuff Anne he has stopped, waiting for instructions from his superior. Fenton is thrown by the confession and begins to bluster, speaking of wasting police time and perverting the course of justice, but Beth now repeats firmly, "I did it."

Sally says to her, "We're not talking about the show you know." because she is taken aback, and thinks that the actress has become confused by the similarity to the nightly performance of what is now taking place in the same scenic surroundings and has started to deliver her usual lines. Could the woman have become so confused by the evening's events that she has lapsed back into her stage role?

"It was because of Bunny," Beth says very quietly.

"Bunny?" several nearby people ask.

"Naomi. My big sister. Everyone called her Bunny."

This last statement slowly penetrates the screaming hysteria in Anne's mind. A bell rings. Adrian had never spoken of it, but a long time ago some in-law once used Naomi and the nickname in a conversation and Adrian had become angry. She is gasping breathlessly from her screaming but she manages to ask, "The girl he killed in the boat?"

Beth nods, "Yes, the girl he killed in the boat. I was only little at the time, but I can still remember. I lost my sister. Mum and Dad never did get over it. And he got away with it. They just said it was an accident. He was never punished. Well he has been now!"

Sally says gently, "Tell us."

"He never recognised me, even though my surname might have been a clue. But the weeks went by and he didn't catch on. I had a bit of difficulty at first getting a bullet, otherwise he'd have paid for what he did much sooner.

"Once I had the bullet it was easy to exchange it for the blank. I had several moments when I was in the prompt side wing alone with the gun. When I reloaded it I dropped the blank, and couldn't find it so I had to give up looking for it. I suppose that was the one you found," she looks at Sally," Then it was easy, but I'm sorry I mistimed the shot. I'd been counting the gap really carefully for a long while before and I was sure I could make it match Sally's shot exactly. But I didn't. And I meant to shoot him in the chest, not the head."

"The recoil pushed your aim up?" Fenton says.

"Yes, and I've hurt my wrist."

Now she has confessed the details come pouring out. The detective is quiet for once, listening to the woman's account. He feels no shame at having wrongly accused Anne. No apology will be offered. The company listens in stunned disbelief as Beth explains in a matter of fact tone how she went to Adrian's dressing room, confronted him and shot him.

"I would have liked to tell him how he'd destroyed Mum and Dad's lives, and mine, as well as killing Bunny, but there wasn't really time. But at the end he knew who I was and that I was going to kill him. Afterwards I slipped back onto stage by running along the backstage passageway and into the scene unnoticed among you all in the wings."

Fenton is almost apologetic as he arrests her. They see a softer side that they had not known existed.

As they start to lead Beth away Julia pushes forward. For a moment it looks as though the policeman will prevent her, but Fenton lets her go up to the prisoner. She doesn't immediately say anything, but reaches out to hand her something. They hear Beth say, "Oh I couldn't!".

"Yes you can," Julia tells her, and they can see Beth is now holding a furry cuddly panda.

As she leaves the stage for the last time Julia shouts after her, "He's called Andy. Andy Panda."

The door leading off the stage swings shut behind Beth.

Chapter 18

Reg is back at the stage door, receiving the dressing room keys as the shell-shocked cast and crew leave. It is nearly dawn and the world outside the theatre is just becoming grey seen through the outside doors. Unlike the usual end of show departures they have all arrived at the lobby more or less together.

"Poor Adrian." one says.

"Poor Beth you mean."

They wrap coats around themselves and there is some quiet conversation as they continue to try to sort out their shocked reactions, and also unlike the usual end of show departures the keys are being given in to Reg faster than he can hang them up. Someone, he doesn't see who in the crowd, hands over two keys. Turning the tags over he sees that one is for Beth Johnstone's room. Sally says, "She wanted me to make sure you got the key back. She says she's sorry not to have cleared out her things before she left."

The low chatter dies as she says this.

Reg says, "Thank you Miss Jenkins, Miss Johnstone was always very thoughtful."

Someone comments, "I still don't see how she got the real bullet."

"Looking back," says Reg, "it might have been my fault."

They pressure him to explain. Sadly, and in the longest comment they have ever heard him make, he tells them about the soldier.

"Apparently he had found out that Adrian had been messing around with his wife. He rolled up here at the stage door one evening demanding to see Mr Birkett. He hadn't come in yet, but Miss Johnstone happened to be arriving at exactly that moment.

Perhaps I shouldn't have introduced her, anyway she got into conversation with him. I don't know exactly what was being said, but they were a bit secretive and she seemed to be agreeing to do something for him. Yesterday, I suppose its the day before now, the army bloke brought a little padded envelope in, addressed to Beth Johnstone. She seemed really excited when I gave it to her. I have a horrible suspicion I may have handed her the bullet."

"Well that explains where she got the live shell from then," Julia says, stooping to pick up an official looking envelope from the grubby floor. No-one pays any attention as he turns it over idly in her hands. Someone has dropped it. She reads the name and address, and slides the contents out. It is a glossy printed leaflet of information, and the phrase.. 'terminal cancer' stands out. 'Poor Beth. I wonder how long she has left,' she thinks, tucking it out of the others' sight in a coat pocket.

Reg finds Rosencrantz is pushing against his leg, he lifts him up, and holding the cat he says "I feel rather guilty."

Sally tells him, "Don't worry Reg, I'm pretty certain that Beth was determined to get revenge on Adrian, It sounds as though other people were too. She'd have found a way to do it even without the bullet, and if she hadn't someone else probably would. We're all just sad that she chose to kill him while the show was still running. Now we're all job hunting because of him."

"I'm not," says Steven,

There are questioning noises from the group.

Julia tells them, "Oh no, no job hunting for the big man here. He got himself a job yesterday and was going to quit the show. So don't blame Adrian for getting shot, and don't blame Beth for pulling the trigger, don't blame the soldier, don't blame Reg for being an unwitting postman. All that has had no effect. Steven here was going to quit anyway. We all know the show would have probably closed as a result. Beth just saved you from getting the blame," she rounds on Steven.

Gradually, amidst recriminations, they all drift out into the cold morning.

Reg sits holding the cat. "I shouldn't wish for things to be more exciting should I?" he asks Rosencrantz.

Also by Cliff Dix
Theatre Wagon
In Which Case
And Burnt The Topless Towers
and
Up The Fire Escape And Through The Kitchens

www.ingramcontent.com/pod-product-compliance
Lightning Source LLC
Chambersburg PA
CBHW070602010526
44118CB00012B/1426